Translating Song

This engaging step-by-step guide prescribes effective strategies and tactics for translating a wide range of songs and other vocal music, from classical to contemporary. Focusing on best practice and with a variety of language examples, the book centres on four key themes:

- translating songs for a range of recipients and within different contexts (*skopos* theory)
- translating songs for reading on paper or on screens (surtitles and subtitles)
- "singable translations" and the Pentathlon Approach
- translating expressive texts.

With a substantial introduction, six insightful chapters, further reading and a glossary of key terms (also available at https://www.routledge.com/9781138641792 and on the Routledge Translation Studies Portal), this lively and clear student-friendly guide is essential for students, researchers and practitioners involved in or studying the practice of translating music. This will also be an engaging read for musicians and all those interested in the study of music.

Peter Low is a senior adjunct fellow in the School of Languages at the University of Canterbury, New Zealand, and a council member of the New Zealand Society of Translators and Interpreters. As a translator of vocal music, he has placed over 150 translations on the LiederNet Archive (www.lieder.net/lieder/), has devised surtitles for six operas and has made singable translations of dozens of songs, both classical and popular.

Translation Practices Explained
Series Editor: Kelly Washbourne

For more information on any of these titles, or to order, please go to www. routledge.com/linguistics

Translation Practices Explained is a series of coursebooks designed to help self-learners and students on translation and interpreting courses. Each volume focuses on a specific aspect of professional translation practice, in many cases corresponding to courses available in translator-training institutions. Special volumes are devoted to well-consolidated professional areas, to areas where labour-market demands are currently undergoing considerable growth and to specific aspects of professional practices on which little teaching and learning material is available. The authors are practicing translators or translator trainers in the fields concerned. Although specialists, they explain their professional insights in a manner accessible to the wider learning public.

These books start from the recognition that professional translation practices require something more than elaborate abstraction or fixed methodologies. They are located close to work on authentic texts, and encourage learners to proceed inductively, solving problems as they arise from examples and case studies.

Each volume includes activities and exercises designed to help learners consolidate their knowledge (teachers may also find these useful for direct application in class, or alternatively as the basis for the design and preparation of their own material). Updated reading lists and website addresses will also help individual learners gain further insight into the realities of professional practice.

Titles in the series:

Conference Interpreting Explained
Roderick Jones

Legal Translation Explained
Enrique Alcaraz and Brian Hughes

Electronic Tools for Translators
Frank Austermuhl

Introduction to Court Interpreting
Holly Mikkelson

Translating Song

Lyrics and texts

Peter Low

Routledge
Taylor & Francis Group

LONDON AND NEW YORK

First published 2017
by Routledge
2 Park Square, Milton Park, Abingdon, Oxon OX14 4RN

and by Routledge
711 Third Avenue, New York, NY 10017

Routledge is an imprint of the Taylor & Francis Group, an informa business

British Library Cataloguing-in-Publication Data
A catalogue record for this book is available from the British Library

Library of Congress Cataloging-in-Publication Data
Names: Low, Peter Alan, author.
Title: Translating song / by Peter Low.
Description: Milton Park, Abingdon, Oxon ; New York, NY :
    Routledge, [2017] | Series: Translation Practices Explained |
    Includes bibliographical references and index.
Identifiers: LCCN 2016020417 | ISBN 9781138641785 (hardback) |
    ISBN 9781138641792 (pbk.) | ISBN 9781315630281 (ebook)
Subjects: LCSH: Language and languages—Rhythm. | Translating and
    interpreting. | Songs—Texts—Translating. | Music and language.
Classification: LCC P311 .L69 2016 | DDC 418/.03782—dc23
LC record available at https://lccn.loc.gov/2016020417

ISBN: 978-1-138-64178-5 (hbk)
ISBN: 978-1-138-64179-2 (pbk)
ISBN: 978-1-3156-3028-1 (ebk)

Typeset in Times New Roman
by Apex CoVantage, LLC

Visit the eResources at https://www.routledge.com/9781138641792

Contents

Figures

Acknowledgements

Many people helped in the creation of this book, knowingly and unknowingly. But any weak content or poor style should be blamed on the author. The individuals I am most grateful to are Anne Kania, Emily Ezust, Joe Flood and Donnalou Stevens.

In part this is a scholarly book. Among scholars I thank Dinda Gorlée and Helen Minors, who critiqued and accepted my articles in their collections, and the various journal editors who enabled me to hone and publish some of my ideas: editors of *Perspectives*, *The Translator*, *Target* and *Babel*.

I thank also other scholars whose writings I have learnt from, notably Johan Franzon, Ronnie Apter and Mark Herman; and other translators of songs I have consulted, including John Glenn Paton, Walter Aue, Pierre Mathé and Erkki Pullinen.

In part this book arises from teaching and practice. I thank students of translation at my own university and in various other countries, notably Seán Ó Luasa of Ireland. I acknowledge many singers and musicians, and my colleagues in the New Zealand Society of Translators and Interpreters.

I also thank the people most involved in the present book project: Kelly Washbourne, Louisa Semlyen and Laura Sandford.

Permissions

For specific permissions to reproduce three copyrighted texts, I thank Warner Chappell Music France for the lyric "Le Fossoyeur" by Georges Brassens; Joe Flood for his singable translation: "The Gravedigger"; and Donnalou Stevens for her lyric "Older Ladies".

Every effort has been made to contact copyright-holders. Please advise the publisher of any errors or omissions, and these will be corrected in subsequent editions.

1 Introduction

Song in human culture

Here are four initial assumptions:

- Vocal music features in the cultural activity of every human society.
- Every song has a verbal as well as a musical dimension.
- A treasury of the world's great songs would include dozens of languages.
- Therefore translating song-lyrics is worth doing.

Music, one of humanity's great arts, is a very international activity. Although those who call it a "universal language" underestimate the differences between varieties, they are not totally wrong. Instrumental music certainly crosses national and linguistic borders, frequently and easily. But most of the music that people most love is vocal music, with or without accompanying instruments. Much of today's huge "music industry" concentrates on songs. And top billing, even when there are gifted instrumentalists, almost always goes to singers.

Almost everyone hears songs every day, at least in electronic form. Cafés and supermarkets pipe them into our ears. In the twenty-first century we have unprecedented access to recorded songs in many languages, from many places, from several past centuries. We can hear them on the radio, YouTube or similar sources; we can watch them on screens; we can read the lyrics online; we can sometimes download the notated music. This has meant a much better availability of different music styles and instruments and greater familiarity with the diversity of songs. In addition, many people walk around with a kind of mental playlist in their heads – an archive of dozens of songs that they can hum or whistle. And some people retain in their memory the lyrics of dozens of songs, or at least the first verse and chorus. Perhaps you, as you read this page, are simultaneously hearing "earworms" – song-tunes wriggling around in your brain whether you like it or not?

All cultures have songs, with words in their own languages: they sing old songs and they make new ones. Song involves people of all ages, towns and countryside, common people and the elite. Singing has often been part of human rituals, by itself or associated with dance and drama. Song can be secular, sacred, sentimental or satirical. Song is part of most people's cultural and linguistic identities, part of many cultural events – weddings, funerals, festivals. While we may associate song with some regions more than others (Italy? Wales?), the truth is that it is everywhere. Most peoples have songs that they hold dear, and many individuals can name "favourite songs", songs which they consider special – highly memorable, sublimely beautiful, unusually moving, uplifting or profound. And the vast and varied corpus of valued song could be considered as a world heritage treasure.

There is the huge variety found in vocal music. The phrase "religious song", for example, covers a vast range. Is there much in common between a Greek Orthodox chant, a five-part Latin Mass, a Handel oratorio with large orchestra, a Salvation Army chorus, an African-American Gospel song and a Christmas Carol piped into a supermarket? Yet those examples do not extend past the frontiers of Christianity – ethnographers could extend the list much further. Even the word "hymn" covers a multitude of sins.

Secular song is even broader: there are songs intended for the tavern or the salon, the cabaret or the music hall, the village fair, the recording studio, the opera house, the rock festival, even the nursery. There are glad songs and sad songs, solo songs and sing-alongs, dancing songs, marching songs, harvest songs, drinking songs, cabaret songs . . . Yet there is always something in common: the components of words, music and performance. Although the author of this book cannot claim familiarity with many kinds of song (few can), he does hope that his book will have wide relevance.

Vocal music is a way of expressing emotion, and has been at many times and in many places – intense and memorable emotion. It is also a way of telling and retelling stories, developing fictional characters, commenting on events, entertaining people and making fun of people. Usually, though not always, the songs' owners value the words as well as the non-vocal elements. Real connoisseurs of the song genre care about the words: they wish for performances that do justice to the verbal component, that truly celebrate the marriage of words and music. (And they think that singers who perform good texts incomprehensibly ought to be forced to sit through ten witty songs played on a saxophone.)

Clearly, the verbal elements of this vocal music cannot cross linguistic borders as readily as the musical elements. This is regrettable and predictable. But it is not irremediable, since the skill of translators can come into play. Indeed translation has long played an important role in the field of music, albeit an often underrated one. (It is common, after all, in international fields of human activity – e.g. science, commerce – for translation to play an important and underrated role.) The main focus of this book is the interface between words and music.

And behind this small focus is a huge concern: one of the continuing problems facing humanity in the twenty-first century is animosity between nations, always compounded by cultural ignorance and usually linked to language differences. Empathy needs to be strengthened, everywhere. Perhaps we need to listen to each other's songs more, both music and words.

Which came first, the words or the music?

Often we don't know. One pattern is "words-first": a musician takes a text by someone else – a text deemed good or promising or sacred – and "sets it" to music, creating a melody inspired by its mood, rhythm and meaning. In these cases the pre-existing words often prompt particular choices of music: contrasts, melodic phrases, percussion, emotional effects of harmony. In nineteenth-century German Lieder, for example, the poems set to music help to explain the principal rhythm, the tempi and tempo-changes of each song, the ways the melody sometimes soars up or plunges down, and the often adventurous musical parts for piano or other instruments. To listen to such songs with no understanding of the words may therefore be puzzling and unsettling, since the words are a key to the music. In the case of a famous Italian aria, Monteverdi's "Lasciatemi morire", the second chord sounded so terribly dissonant that one British editor amended the bass-line in order to "correct it". Yet that striking dissonance was inspired by the character's cry of pain, meaning: "Let me die". The pre-existing words explained the unusual music – as the editor ought to have known.

Another pattern is "music-first", where a promising melody is the partial inspiration for the lyric. Would you have guessed that the Beatles' classic "Yesterday" began as a tune, for which the words were subsequently invented? And that the first phrase they thought of was "Scrambled Eggs"? Then there is a third pattern: a singer-songwriter develops the music and the lyric in tandem, zigzagging from one to the other. During the process both words and melody can be very fluid, until they come together.

For translators, fortunately, these patterns make little difference. We can approach the lyrics as finished artefacts, and try to make them serviceable in a new context.

Introductory questions and answers

What is this book about?

It's about translating, in the sense of the interlingual transfer of content, especially meaning, from one language to another. This is a relatively narrow definition, yet a normal one in the translating profession. The book will devote a lot of space to the forms of decision-making and problem-solving that all translators engage in: appreciating the original text in the context of its own language and culture, generating options in another language and choosing the optimal phrase to satisfy a specific purpose – with this difference that it looks at texts not often discussed in translation literature: song-lyrics. Song-lyric is a catch-all term for any text sung in any vocal music. This book asks frequent questions about the purpose of translating a song-lyric. Is the translation intended for reading on page or screen, for example, or for singing in the target language?

It is a "How-To" book. Unlike some past discussions of song-translations, its focus is not on describing and analysing how people in the past have translated and adapted vocal music, but on suggesting strategies and tactics for doing it well in the future. Yet these prescriptions cannot be dogmatic ones. Sometimes the prescription reads more like: "Here are some good questions to ask yourself." Whereas for the translation of official documents – or legal or scientific texts – there exist protocols and codes of ethics, there is nothing like an established "best practice" for song-texts. On the contrary, there has been a confusing freedom of practice and terminology in this area.

Who is this book for?

One group is students of translation. Not just those who have English as their first language – in the US, UK or elsewhere – but students who can read English, whether living in Europe, South America, India, China or elsewhere. Song-lyrics are not typical texts, in any language: they are creative, and often playful. Investigating their quirks may provide a fun alternative to the generally informative texts that you work on and may well help to enlarge your "box of tools" for solving translation problems.

The book is also aimed at the following: professional translators who sometimes encounter vocal texts; researchers into song or translation or inter-cultural exchange; singers and amateur wordsmiths interested in the challenge of translating songs; and fans of vocal music generally.

What kinds of song?

All kinds of songs in all languages – secular and sacred, sentimental and satirical, old songs in dead languages, new songs in dialect: the whole alphabet from A to Z (from air to zarzuela, through blues, carols, epithalamiums, folksongs, glees . . .). This may seem ambitious, yet it is justified, because all songs, despite the huge diversity of genres in many languages and cultures, always have a musical component and a verbal component. Wordless chants are not songs in the fullest sense: the beautiful *vocalises* of (say) Fauré, Rachmaninov and Villa-Lobos merely use the human voice as a melody instrument. Songs need voices singing words.

Optionally, songs may also involve musical instruments, and usually they do (e.g. one guitar). Optionally, they can be published in notation on a page; yet the "sheet music" is not really the music. Optionally, they may be accompanied by visual elements, ranging from simple gestures by the performers to elaborate video clips. Yet these visual things are adjuncts: they are not intrinsic to the songs. Although retailers may well choose to separate items into such categories as pop/hip-hop or gospel/jazz/blues etc., those are merely sub-genres.

From the standpoint of translating, two notable features about this genre are:

- the variety of specific purposes for which a translation might be sought (see chapter 3), and
- the very tight constraints imposed by one of these purposes, namely when the translation must itself be singable (see chapters 5 and 6).

Besides, although the term "song" is not used for extended vocal performances like musicals or operas, much of this book is applicable to those musical-verbal hybrids – and to choral music as well, whether or not the choir item is obviously a song. This book is concerned not only with song-lyrics written as such and poems later set to music, but also with other kinds of text used in various forms of singing.

All good songs marry verbal communication to musical communication. The best are more than worthy to be carried and enhanced by music. Some people might argue that the song-lyrics in certain sub-genres are weak and not worth translating, and they are sometimes right; but this book prefers to concentrate on how to do it.

Its emphasis, admittedly, will be on songs where the words are relatively interesting, what jazz-singer Malcolm McNeill has called "songs with staying power". But in all genres we can find strong, well-crafted songs with words that play and don't plod. This book offers tools and questions that might help you to translate whatever song you wish to translate, whatever your motivation and whatever your purpose. The tools might not be helpful with every song, but the questions are likely to be useful.

Now a little disclaimer: while discussing translations and adaptations (chapter 7 will attempt to distinguish between these), this book will not examine "Replacement Texts". These are cases where a song-tune has crossed a language-border and acquired *a new set of words having no connection with the original words and meanings.* This phenomenon is fairly common, both within languages and across languages. For example a sacred song may be given secular words or vice versa. The new texts are not "translations" because nothing verbal has been "carried over" (*übersetzt* in German), and therefore the resulting musico-verbal creation ought not to be called "the same song". This practice of writing new words for existing tunes is a legitimate cultural phenomenon, but it is not translating or adapting.

It's really about classical songs, highbrow stuff, isn't it?

No. Chapter 3 concerns the situation where songs are performed in the SL, and this tends to happen more with highbrow songs. But this tendency is far from universal (for example pop songs are sung in English by Chinese or Brazilian groups). Conversely, chapters 5 and 6 concern the situation when songs are performed in the TL, and this tends to occur more with popular songs. Yet some classical songs are often sung in translation – e.g. those of Tchaikovsky – and this option ought to be used more. Besides, the dichotomy between highbrow and lowbrow, between "serious music" and "popular music", is often exaggerated.

What do those acronyms mean? The first of many, no doubt!

Actually there are only four:

SL for source language, ST for source text,
TL for target language, TT for target text.

These are used a great deal, admittedly. And there is a compelling reason: the book claims to be relevant to any language. Though it may seem at times to concern one language-pair, it aspires to discuss strategies and tactics that could be applied to translating in any direction between any pair of languages.

If it were just about translating in one direction from one particular language, I would be saying something like "the French text" and "the English text", since there lies my greatest competence. But no, it attempts to have a much wider applicability, and for this reason it speaks of transforming a source text (ST) in a source language (SL) into a target text (TT) in a target language (TL).

Then why are so many of the examples in English?

It is sensible nowadays for an international book to be published in English. As a consequence, this is the one language understandable by every reader. Besides, the most widely diffused pop-music in recent decades has originated in the US and the UK.

But even the pages devoted to the specificities of English (as a SL and as a TL) are intended to highlight a general principle, namely that *every language has its particular features*, all of which could be explored in their own terms. Furthermore, the book is not meant only for native English-speakers. Many readers will have English as their second or third language. That is why the term "foreign language" will be avoided – foreign to whom?

So here's a book trying to talk about general principles. We – author and readers – will need to remind ourselves that general principles cannot be based only on one or two languages or language-pairs.

Why are many of the examples chosen from the past?

Why not? A general principle can be illustrated from any time or place. Believe it or not, vocal music did exist before YouTube, and song-translating has been done for ages! Vocal music in English goes back centuries, and that of Shakespeare's time is of high quality. Besides, this author prefers to limit the number of copyright permissions sought and to choose examples from the public domain. Actually, a few don't come from real songs – but whether real lyrics or not, they are words and phrases of the kind one might encounter in translating songs.

But the music is more important than the words, isn't it?

Generally speaking, yes. Most listeners focus on the music, at least on first encounter. There are many ways in which the musical dimension of a song can dominate the words – strong rhythms, percussive effects, instrumental riffs, striking harmonies, vocal timbres, changes in orchestration. The magic of good music is such that even if you can hear the words, the musical elements dominate. I might get some pleasure from (say) a Hungarian song whose words I don't understand, whereas I wouldn't watch a Hungarian movie unless there are subtitles to convey the verbal dimension. In songs the music is more interesting, on average.

But plenty of songs are not average. Some have awful words that ought to be scrapped (national anthems, perhaps?); some are short and repetitive, accompanied by loud dance rhythms which make following the words difficult, and with a content dominated by clichés about dating and love; some are so weak that their success is due only to a charismatic performer. Conversely, many songs rely heavily on words, in order to tell stories or jokes; and the particular *frisson* of the most heart-breaking songs arises from the mysterious marriage of a verbal phrase and a musical one. Some have survived solely through their texts – such as the ancient Greek lyric poems whose music was lost long ago. Usually the words matter, at least to some extent, or at least they mattered to the creators – the songwriters, poets and composers in question. The relative importance of words and music is discussed below under the heading "Logocentric?"

Translating song lyrics is difficult!

OK, so nobody will use this book! After all, no one ever attempts mental challenges like jigsaws or cryptic crosswords or chess puzzles or Scrabble problems or fiendish Sudokus, do they? But consider the English proverb: "Calm seas don't make good mariners."

The vast field of song-translating

Translators are not "unsung heroes" – not if you consider how often their TTs are literally sung.

Many people associate a song with a particular performer – often a singer-songwriter – and this is normal enough. Yet the song is not simply that performance: it has a notional existence independent of any individual performance or recording. The same song can be sung at different pitches, with different accompanying instruments and somewhat different speeds. Can songs be sung in different languages? We know that they can be, because they are! Yes, songs are sung in translation, a lot of songs, very frequently. Translating is done, and is done successfully.

Consider major works of music theatre. Many Broadway musicals are adapted into various languages, including French, German and Swedish. Sondheim's *Into the Woods* has been performed in Spanish and Catalan. *Fiddler on the Roof* has been performed in Hebrew. The rock opera *Evita*, originally in English, has been performed in Spanish and Portuguese. Conversely, the 1980 musical *Les Misérables* has had more performances in English than in the original French.

As for operas, dozens, if not hundreds have been sung in translation. It used to be common for Italian operas (Verdi, Rossini etc.) to be performed in German, French or English. Tchaikovsky's *Evgeny Onegin* can still be heard in English and French. A few operas even had their first performances in translated versions, e.g. *Samson et Dalila* by Saint-Saëns. Nowadays, however, most translations of opera are done not for singing but for reading on surtitle or subtitle screens (see chapter 3).

Operas were often performed in translation.

This page (Figure 1.1) comes from a nineteenth-century British collection of arias, intended to help amateurs sing and play. It records on paper an aria by Gounod, with words by Barbier and Carré after the German of Goethe. In this piano-vocal score you see the French text underlaid to the tune and sandwiched between two singable versions into English and Italian, anonymous.

The English version is not so much a translation as an adaptation. And look at bar 6 – the English adds a syllable at the start (suppressing a slur) and then subtracts one (adding a slur not present in the French).

When all was young

(Quando a te Lieta)

(FAUST)

Figure 1.1 Faust, from a piano score of arias

And what of hit songs? It is common for a successful song to be "covered" several times, that is, re-recorded by another artist with modifications to the music and sometimes the words. This may seem strange, since the hit doubtless owed its success to an excellent performance, which the covers fail to match. Sometimes they disrespect the songs, annoy the original artists and breach copyright laws. But covers are numerous, and some of them, unsurprisingly, have been translations.

Thus a hit like Leonard Cohen's "Hallelujah", in addition to many covers in English, has been sung in several languages. Audiences are often not told that they are hearing a translation or adaptation. It is well known that some of the songs sung in English by ABBA were born in Swedish. But not everyone realises that several "Elvis Presley songs" were originally in Italian – e.g. "Surrender" (1960) began life as "Torna a Sorrento" (1902) – or that the original words to "My Way" (made famous by Sinatra) were in French "Comme d'habitude". Similarly, "The Girl from Ipanema" began life in Brazilian Portuguese, as a song by Vinicius de Moraes and Tom Jobim.

QUIZ. Which of the following statements is not true?

The musical *Cats* has been adapted into several languages including Hungarian.

The French opera *Carmen* has been translated into Xhosa.

The "Hallelujah Chorus", which uses phrases of the King James *Bible* (translated from Greek), was subsequently translated, with the help of Luther's *Bible*, into the native language of the composer Händel.

The British hit "It's a Long Way to Tipperary" (1912) had travelled so far by 1915 that it was sung in New Zealand Māori as "He roa te wā ki Tipirere".

The Elvis Presley song "Wooden Heart" has been translated into Latin as "Cor ligneum".

The jaunty *chanson* "Aux Champs-Élysées", a homage to the famous Paris avenue, originated as a British song: "Waterloo Road".

Bob Dylan's song "A Hard Rain's A-Gonna Fall" was a big hit in Israel in its Hebrew version.

"Pop Goes the Weasel" has been adapted into Modern Greek and sung on the BBC with English subtitles.

An adaptation of "Give Peace a Chance" (John Lennon/Plastic Ono Band) was a big hit at the Klingon Convention in 2017.

Many other performers in English have included translations or adaptations in their repertoire, for example Johnny Mercer, Rod McKuen, Scott Walker. Few people are aware that Pete Seeger's famous "Where Have All the Flowers Gone?" took some lines from the traditional Cossack folksong "Koloda-Duda". Conversely, many songs are translated out of English. For example "La Quête", recognised in France as a "Jacques Brel song", originated in an American musical, *The Man of La Mancha*. In recent decades, the vogue for US and British work means that many performers elsewhere chose to adapt it into Spanish, Russian or Chinese versions (or else to sing it in fractured English to audiences that maybe don't care). Not a few popular performers sing or record in more than one language: Björk, Céline Dion, Mariah Carey . . . In Asia, meanwhile, singable translations are made from Persian into Arabic, from Bengali into Hindi, from Japanese into Korean.

Although making singable translations is not easy, it cannot be claimed that the difficulty has great deterrent value – indeed the fine but tricky French texts of Brassens and Brel have tempted many translators in many countries (Brassens 1992). In addition, non-singable translations have been made in their thousands, and dozens are made every day, for example through fansubbing (subtitling of videos by amateur fans).

Logocentric?

Do the words matter in the songs of David Bowie or Michael Jackson? Or those of Taylor Swift or Justin Bieber? Or Adele or Lorde or Ricky Martin or Tim Minchin or the Flight of the Conchords?

Questions of that kind are crude, because they seem to call for a yes/no answer. A more discerning question is "How important are the words in these songs, compared with the music?" But even this question calls for some sort of averaging (40% perhaps) across a large number of works. What the translator really needs to ask is a question focused on the individual case: "How important are the words of this particular song I am tackling?"

The term "logocentric" means word-centred (from the Greek *logos*). Some people use it to characterise the general view that in vocal music the words matter most, and use the term "musico-centric" for the contrary view. But this is altogether too simplistic, despite the airing it has had, for example in the Strauss opera *Capriccio*.

Instead we can apply the term "logocentric" to actual songs where the words matter more, and "musico-centric" to the others. An extreme case of a logocentric song is Noel Coward's "Mrs Worthington" – which would be a good recitation piece without any music. An extremely musico-centric song is Rossini's "Cat Duet" where the only word sung is "Miau" (is that Italian or French?). Between those extremes there lies a long continuum.

Here is the lyric of a song that is relatively logocentric:

Older Ladies by Donnalou Stevens *(reproduced by kind permission)*

Well, I ain't 16, not a beauty queen.
My eyes are baggin' and my skin is saggin',
And if that's the reason that you don't love me,
Then maybe that's not love.

Well I ain't 20 either and I don't care neither.
My hair is gray and I like it that way.
And if that's the reason that you don't love me,
Then maybe that's not love.

If you don't think I rock, well we ain't gonna roll.
If you don't think I hung the moon, my hot just turned to cold.
If you want a younger model, I wish you well, sweet pea.
'cause if you can't see what it is you have,
Then you ain't having me.

I got cellulite and achin' feet,
And my thighs kinda jiggle when I giggle or wiggle,
And if that's the reason that you don't love me,
Then maybe that's not love.

My tummy ain't tucked or liposucked.
It's a little poochy, but I still Hoochy Koochy,
And if that's the reason that you don't love me,
Then maybe that's not love.

See, I'm no longer desperate. I'll only have a man,
If he has the smarts to see how hot that I still am.
If you want a younger model, I wish you well, sweet pea.
If you can't see what it is you have,
Then you ain't having me.

Older ladies, older ladies, older ladies . . . are DIVINE!
Well I gotta chicken neck and I love it, by heck,
It makes a double chin whenever I grin,
And if that's the reason that you don't love me,
Then maybe that's not love.

I got saggy breasts that droop from my chest,
Pert near down all the way to my nest,
And if that's the reason that you don't love me,
Then maybe that's not love.

If you don't think I rock, well we ain't gonna roll.
If you don't think I hung the moon, my hot just turned to cold.
If you want a younger model, I wish you well, sweet pea.
'cause if you can't see what it is you've got,
You ain't getting me.

Older ladies, older ladies, older ladies . . . are DIVINE!
Older ladies, older ladies, older ladies . . . what are we ladies? We're DIVINE!

That song "went viral" in 2014–15, mostly because of the words. But the music is stylish too, the performance is lively . . . and the video puts icing on the cake. You can view it on YouTube (just Google "Donnalou Older Ladies"). Logocentric and well crafted, it surely merits translating, probably in a singable version.

Musico-centric songs tend to be more numerous and certainly have less difficulty in crossing language borders, because logocentric songs are too word-focused to be appreciated as pure melody. This distinction is useful because the songs most worth translating are logocentric ones, those that might be too shallow without the verbal dimension.

Near the musico-centric pole of the continuum lie Italian operatic arias: they may have very few words and repeat some phrases eight times in a number of acrobatic ways. Sometimes the words would be very trite without the melody; indeed Rossini once claimed he could make an aria out of a laundry list, presumably an Italian one. In the sacred repertoire, most settings of the Latin Benedictus or the Greek Kyrie emphasise the music much more than the words. The same could be said of many tango songs: the lyrics are subordinate, adjuncts to the emotional music.

Conversely, near the logocentric pole of the continuum lie the witty numbers of Ira Gershwin or Cole Porter (such as "Let's Do It"), or Tom Lehrer or Stephen Sondheim. A notable logocentric translation out of French is "Master of the House" from *Les Misérables.* The French *chanson* tradition of singers like Edith Piaf and Léo Ferré tends towards the logocentric end of the continuum. Here's one test: would you invite foreign visitors to listen to these songs if they could not understand the verbal dimension?

A clear case is satire. Nobody can appreciate satirical songs without grasping the words. They are what count most. And it follows that you can't make good translations of satirical songs unless your strategy is focused on the words – their sense and their bite – even at the expense of their musical integrity.

Apart from satire, some other kinds of songs that are generally logocentric are:

- narrative songs – the story is carried by the words
- comic songs – music can aid jokes but cannot crack them
- dramatic songs – when events are happening, e.g. in a musical
- protest songs – music can aid a message but not state one
- dialogue songs – where one singer delivers words for two characters. Two traditional examples are "Where Have You Been, Billy Boy?" and "Soldier, Soldier, Will You Marry Me?"

In addition we can mention "first-person character songs", dramatic monologues where the singer delivers the words of a fictional character: "I am" . . . the Devil, or the soldier Zangra, or Henry VIII, or a dying man, or a statue on a war memorial, or a teenager in New York, or a middle-aged lawyer, or a young soldier, or a meerkat, or a chimney, or a teapot or an ex-horse. Most of those examples come from Jacques Brel. Such songs need the audience to follow the words.

This variation applies even to songs from a single source: within a single show, such as *The Gondoliers* (Gilbert and Sullivan) we can find a melodious musico-centric song "Take a Pair of Sparkling Eyes" and a patter-song beginning "In enterprise of martial kind", where the focus is clearly on the clever lyric – few listeners ignorant of English could enjoy the boring repeated music of that. So a single work has numbers ranging across the continuum.

Indeed even a single song may shift between logocentric and musico-centric sections. It often happens in Broadway musicals that a soloist's "big melodic number" is preceded by an introduction which is much more wordy. This applies also to some songs that have repeated refrains: the verses (the varying stanzas) have more verbal content, whereas the repeated refrains add little to the meaning. A good example is Gershwin's "It Ain't Necessarily So", where each verse is about a different *Bible* story.

We find a similar shift in traditional opera, where the big solo songs are called "arias". These are the bits often performed and recorded as "opera highlights". Arias typically focus on the music and the virtuosity of the singer, the number of acrobatic ways in which a phrase can be sung. Often the words would be very trite without the melody. Yet musico-centric arias often have preludes called "recitatives", where the singer delivers a lot of words without very much melody. Thus Mozart's "Se vuol ballare" is preceded by a recitative "Bravo signor padrone", and Verdi's aria "Ernani, involami" by a recitative "Surta è la notte". Recitatives are scored lightly by the composer and sung in a kind of "half-speaking" technique. In an extreme case, "E la solita storia del pastore" (Cilea), the first 16 syllables of text are spoken at the same pitch – so it's obviously not about the music! Recitatives may form lengthy dialogues, and at times they carry much of the opera's storyline. They are much more logocentric than arias.

All this is relevant to translating, of course, particularly for singable translations where the constraints can lead to changes of meaning (see chapters 5 and 6). It explains the hybrid option chosen by some opera productions: they keep the pretty arias in Italian while presenting the recitatives in the language of the audience. This option certainly works well for a comic opera like Rossini's *Barbiere di Siviglia*, where much of the humour lies in the recitatives. It makes excellent sense to use the TL for these wordy sections, whereas the case for keeping the arias in the original Italian is strong. And in general you should translate phrases in terms of *what those words are doing* at that point of the work, whether they are providing information, humour, emotion or whatever.

Recitatives are found also in oratorio, notably in Bach's great works the *Matthäus-Passion* and the *Johannes-Passion*. Since the narrative sections are taken directly from the gospels, the tenor performing them is actually called the "Evangelist". Here Bach's music sets Luther's *Bible* translation, but many performances outside Germany use a translation into the language of the audience – who are seen as the congregation of faithful come to hear again the Passion Story. A good example in English is the *St John Passion* published by Novello in 1999 (translation by Neil Jenkins).

You will be less motivated to translate a song-lyric if the words are not good and important. Here are some questions that may be relevant:

- Does the song tell a story? (e.g. the ballad "Polly Oliver")
- Does the song tell verbal jokes?
- Does it use a rich vocabulary?
- Was the text written by a famous poet (e.g. *Cats* by Eliot)?
- Are there lots of different verses?
- Are the words sung with sincerity, as if the singer believed them?
- Are they audible over the percussion and other instruments?
- Are they clear enough to transcribe?
- Was it originally sung in the language of the audience?
- Will your target audience be interested in the combined musico-verbal effect?

Some Musical Terminology — and a Christmas Song!

Here is a vocal score for a four-part choir. "Ding Dong! Merrily" counts as sacred music, because of the words; yet the tune was first published as a secular French dance (1588).

This is a strophic song, because its three verses (or "strophes") are each sung to the same music. **Strophic songs** differ from **through-composed songs,** in which every phrase has new music.

Many strophic songs have a **refrain** – the same words repeated at the end of each verse. With this song, unusually, the refrain is in a different language. The English words (by G.R. Woodward 1848–1934) include deliberate archaisms –"ye", "sungen". The Latin words are from Luke's Gospel as translated out of Greek by Jerome, the patron saint of translators.

Another huge contrast between verse and refrain is that the English verse receives a **syllabic setting,** while the refrain uses **melisma.**

A melisma is when one syllable is sung to more than one note. The most common melismas have two or three notes, linked with curving marks called **slurs.** Here, however, the syllable GLO- has a very long melisma: in the top line it has more than 30 notes before the Latin word finally ends, with -RIA. Conversely, the English verses have no melismas at all: only one note per syllable (as is common in many simple songs).

This is a relatively **musico-centric** song, since the verses are merely quaint while the refrain is musically glorious. If you were asked to make a singable version of this, you should retain the Latin refrain and should probably treat the verses freely, reducing the archaism and richness of rhyme, yet striving to make it sound good in the TL.

DING DONG! MERRILY ON HIGH

Tune, *Branle de l'official*
from Thoinot Arbeau's *Orckesograpkt'e*, 1588
(C.W.)

G. R. Woodward

Figure 1.2 Christmas song – *Ding Dong!*

These are only indicative questions. But positive answers strengthen the case for translation, and too many negatives weaken it.

Clearly some songs lose a lot if performed instrumentally – without the words – or if sung in a language foreign to the audience. Purely instrumental renditions of popular songs will prove a failure if subtracting the words is too costly. This is particularly true of humour, which works best with quick impact and good timing. A good experiment would be to rehearse the old part-song by Niclas Piltz "Die Weiber mit den Flöhen" and then perform it twice, first to an audience with no understanding of the words, and then to an audience of Germans. Would the verbal dimension make a difference? Certainly, it means: "The women who have fleas"! But serious songs need their words too: some of them contain surprises (weird harmonies) and unexpected transitions (e.g. from slow to fast) which make very little sense in isolation from the text.

There are various ways of helping the verbal elements to cross language borders, and many translations don't try to be singable (see chapter 3).

The distant origins of this book

Growing up in the English-speaking world, though distant from London and New York, I heard a lot of Anglo-American popular music. This was an age of radio and record players, before the Internet existed. A little jazz and Latin-American music was played, but nothing really Asian or African. Most of the vocal music was in English. Nobody told me that the words of "Fascination" (sung by Nat King Cole and others) were originally in French. I was also initiated, despite low birth and income, into the highbrow European music of earlier centuries, what was loosely called "classical music".

Like other children, I was expected to learn songs. The tunes were fun, but some of the words struck me as archaic and obscure, especially those in nursery rhymes. Although my city was virtually monolingual, some songs were in strange languages: Latin, French, Maori, Scots. I soon preferred words that made sense, songs that were not just pretty tunes but that also "said something".

At the church we attended, the hymns were all in English. Protestant Christianity has a strong tradition of using the language of the people (more so than Catholicism, Islam or Judaism). But I later learnt that some of them had originally been in Latin, German or Welsh. That was my first encounter with bad translations: "Stille Nacht/Silent Night" might be a nice carol, but hey, if the English solution was "round yon virgin" then there was something wrong with the question! Another puzzle was "The Lord's my shepherd": we sang – as some people still do – about "pastures green" and "the quiet waters by" (what do they buy?).

This text is an odd kind of translation: originating as an ancient Hebrew psalm, unrhymed, it had been put into good English by King James's team in 1611 and then mangled by a Scottish wordsmith whose crazy strategy was to put the same words in the wrong order for the sake of iambic rhythms and perfect rhymes.

Then my sister starting singing lessons, from a teacher steeped in the European tradition dominated by Italy and Germany. Soon I heard some German songs being sung in English versions which didn't really work as English texts. Some other people agreed. I have subsequently met singers who refuse to ever sing translations of classical songs. "This needs to be heard in the original Italian," they said, "a translation can't ever satisfy." A few even argued that song-translating is impossible. This extreme view is not really tenable, but the ready availability of amateurish and incompetent song-translations explains how it arose.

Later my father obtained a recording with extracts from a well-translated operetta: *Orpheus in the Underworld* (Offenbach, as performed by the Sadler's Wells company). Here was an irreverent French pantomime about ancient gods, with English words that did work well: clever and humorous words which W. S. Gilbert himself could have been proud of. Whether this version was a close translation of the libretto I couldn't then judge, but it certainly fulfilled its function very well: it amused and delighted. It must have proceeded from good strategies well implemented.

Chapters to follow

Chapters 2 and 4 will focus on two constant aspects of translating: the "upstream problems" posed by the source texts and the "downstream problems" involved in creating the target text in the target language. These focus particularly, but not exclusively, on the specific genre of song-lyrics.

Chapters 3, 5 and 6 will concentrate on issues of *skopos*: the purpose which the ST is meant to fulfil. Chapter 3 concerns non-singable translations: a number of ways in which a TT may be linked to a song sung in the SL. Chapters 5 and 6 concern singable translation and propose the "pentathlon principle" as a practical tool for improving and evaluating this tricky task.

Chapter 7 focuses on adaptations, which have been common ways of carrying songs across language borders. They are sometimes called "free translations".

***

Exercises

This chapter printed the words of "Older Ladies" by Donnalou Stevens. Look at them again, and consider these groups of questions:

(A) To what extent do you think its success was based on the lyric, the music or the video featuring Hillary Clinton and a chicken? Do you think it was more popular with women or men, with young people or older people? How much would it be enjoyed by people who understand little or no English?

(B) How well do you understand it, really? Does "pert" mean "pert" or what? Does a "younger model" mean a new car, a live mannequin or what? Does the phrase "hung the moon" mean anything at all?

(C) If you had to translate it into the other language you work with, what is the main thing you would not want to omit? Does the "I" mean the song-writer as an individual or as a type? Who is denoted by the "you"? Is it OK to translate "ladies" with the most common word for "women"? What TL word or expression would you choose for "sweet pea", or "hot", or "nest" or "Hoochy-Koochy"?

(D) On top of those linguistic issues, there are cultural ones. The song comes from California, where a popular song-and-movie culture raves about youth and sex and feminine beauty. Given that background, what serious point is the song making about social norms? Could a translated or adapted version make a similar point in another cultural context?

(E) One very tricky detail is a kind of pun. In the chorus, the words "older ladies" sound rather like "yodelaydeez", and the vocal line suddenly leaps up in a sort of yodel – an imitation of Tyrolean Jodelmusik. This play on words is reinforced on the videoclip by images of people wearing Lederhosen in a meadow. Could you replicate that in another language? Or could you permit your TT to retain those two English words "older ladies"?

(F) Do you have the skill and patience to translate the lyric?

Further reading

Of general relevance are two articles in the *New Grove Dictionary of Music and Musicians* (2001, London & New York, Macmillan): "Song" vol. XXIII, 704–716, and "Popular Music" vol. XX, 128–166.

Two major scholarly collections concerning vocal translation are: Gorlée, Dinda (ed) (2005) *Song and Significance: Virtues and Vices of Vocal Translation*, Amsterdam & New York, Rodopi. This contains Dinda Gorlée's own impressive article "Singing on the Breath of God", concerning hymns and translation (pp. 17–101). She found that 20 per cent of the hymns in an 1871 Anglican collection were translations.

Minors, Helen Julia (ed) (2012) *Music, Text and Translation*. London, Bloomsbury.

Also very relevant is:

Apter, Ronnie & Herman, Mark (2016) *Translating for Singing – The Theory, Art and Craft of Translating Lyrics*, London, Bloomsbury.

References

"Brassens (1992)" refers to: *Traduire et interpréter Georges Brassens*: 91–112. This collective volume is nos 22/1–2 & 23/1 (1992–1993) of *Equivalences*, Bruxelles, Institut supérieur de traducteurs et interprètes: 91–112. The articles (some in English) cite translations of Brassens songs into English, German, Swedish, Czech, Dutch, Italian etc.

For Jacques Brel, similarly, the website www.brelitude.net shows how dozens of Brel songs have been translated into dozens of languages. Clearly many performers loved the words of these songs and wanted their audiences to really understand them.

2 Looking closely at the source text

What features can make songs hard to translate?

Upstream issues

Any kind of text can pose problems for translators. Nobody has tried to make a complete list of traps that may be found in a ST, and if anyone did someone else would want to add to it! This chapter looks only at a few of them, omitting many significant ones – such as acronyms, which are less of a plague in songs than in official reports.

The problems found in songs are characteristic of literary texts, especially of poems. This is because good lyrics tend to be more subtle and poetic than prose. One virtue of this book may be that the genre it examines is very unlike the standard non-fiction documents that feature in translation courses. You therefore need to give the lyric a very careful reading, so as to understand and appreciate its meaning, its grammar and also the stylistic choices made by the writer. This may well put pressure on your knowledge of the SL. You should also take account of the alliance with music, which is of course a defining feature of song-texts.

Some are far removed from ordinary communicative texts, because they play with language. As one song-translator says: "Often the poet uses a poem to express the unsayable. To do so he diverts words from their original sense, he forges new words, he exploits and sometimes abuses figures of style (often allegory, personification, metaphor etc.) . . . There are also poets of humour or of the absurd" (Mathé 2015). These will certainly prove difficult.

Are song-lyrics poems? There is certainly an overlap. Some song-texts began life as printed poems. And most can be described as "oral poetry", resembling in particular the kinds of lyric poems that are best read aloud. One may even choose to classify all song-texts as poetry – though one should then admit that not many are excellent poems. It has even been said that "a lyric without its musical clothes is a scrawny creature and should not be allowed to parade naked across a printed page" – and that is the view of a renowned lyricist, Alan Jay Lerner (1978: 6).

It is more useful, for translators, to put song-lyrics in the general category of "expressive texts" and distinguish them from "informative texts" and "operative texts", using the terminology of Katharina Reiss (1971/2001). This distinction leads us to focus not on what information a song conveys to its audience but on how it expresses the inspiration of the creator(s). This approach aligns song-lyrics with personal expression of other kinds – poems, diaries, personal letters – in which the focus is not on the raw content. This is true even when the song-text uses a fictional character saying "I", since dramatic monologues and anecdotes are expressive texts too. The fact that songs are not principally written to convey facts means that your efforts need to be far-ranging if you are to successfully replicate their verbal actions, to *do in the TL* whatever complex things the song-lyrics were *doing in the SL*.

There is great diversity in what the authors of song-lyrics might be doing. Some are lamenting, some are rejoicing. We can find cases where they are serenading, pleading, teasing, explaining, narrating, alluding, cajoling, ironising, satirising, insulting, joking etc. Seldom do they focus on informing their listeners, since that is something that other genres do better. And what is the song – words and music together – trying to *make the audience do*? To make them laugh, make them cry, make them relax or what? A translator who misjudges this is hardly likely to do a good job.

Besides, song-texts are oral texts. What you may see on paper is only a written transcript of the song-lyric. Just as a printed page of music is not "the music" but a mere shorthand notation of it (what the Germans call "die Noten"), so a printed song-lyric is essentially a readable "score" intended for an oral performance. Therefore your assessment of what the ST is *doing or trying to do* needs to be based on the music as well as the words. Consider what the music can tell you about the tone of the words – you might translate them differently if the music is fast rather than slow, if it makes them sound frivolous rather than solemn. Exactly how the words fit with the music matters less – unless you are making a singable translation (see chapters 5 and 6). Some song-lyrics postdate the music, in which case the music is a major source of the text. But even when the text began life as a poem on a page, what you are translating is *the text as a song-lyric*, and so you need to take account of the musician's interpretation of the words – commenting on certain words, for example by the musical effects sometimes called "word-painting". Peter Newmark has said that the words of vocal music "must be interpreted alongside its musical language, namely its pitch contours, its harmonic setting, its rhythmic and metrical characteristics as well as its performative features (the articulation, dynamics and expression projected by the singer)" (2012: 61). That quotation mentions not only elements created by the composer (e.g. high notes, jerky rhythms) but also the performer's contribution to the whole.

It is certainly not good practice to translate a song-lyric without hearing the song. This is especially true for the work of singer-songwriters, whose performances have special authority, because they know better than anyone else what the song means, or at least what it was intended to mean. Although we can't always believe everything that these artists say about their works' meaning, we can expect their performances to shed some light. It would be very strange for anyone to translate songs by a famous group like Queen without watching on video the performances of Freddie Mercury.

What does Mick Jagger mean by "I can't get no satisfaction"? Is that disappointment, frustration or anger? Hear the performance and you'll know! In fact the double negative gives a clue: this is not standard English (in which two negatives would make a positive). Therefore you should not translate as if he had sung "I cannot get satisfaction"; you should choose a stronger, more colloquial option, if you can find one in your TL.

One translator, Walter Aue, has said of some German Lieder: "It is impossible to translate the text as if one had never heard the song. The melody and its expressions plays in the head [. . .] I tried to translate 'the song' rather than 'the lyrics'. This takes a much longer time than the original text and is quite a bit more difficult" (2015). And what if several musicians made settings of the same poetic text – a piece of Shakespeare, perhaps, or Goethe? This could well affect your translation of the lyric. The Verlaine poem "Le ciel est par-dessus le toit" is certainly darker and more anguished in Fauré's setting than in Hahn's.

Even the best translations fall short of perfection. But all good translations are superior to bad ones in respect to (a) showing a deep understanding of the ST, with its original context and purpose, and (b) transferring or replicating all its important features, sometimes at the expense of its incidental details.

Imagine a news article in which you notice alliteration between a long adjective and its noun, for example the phrase "geriatric generals". Whether or not you think that effect was deliberate, you should normally – in journalistic prose – translate the meaning of the adjective. In song, however, which is an oral genre not focused on information, you may well judge that sound-effect to be the most important feature and choose to replicate it through an alliterative adjective with a less precise meaning.

Imagine you are subtitling a video of a formal speech made by someone who stutters. You should ignore the extraneous consonants. But where they are intentional – as in the songs "K-K-K-Katie" and "The Stuttering Lovers" (Hughes) – that effect is a deliberate gimmick, indeed it is a key to the whole song. This may apply to other cases where mispronunciation is a salient feature of a song.

The outer characteristics of song-lyrics

They are oral texts, and as such they differ greatly from written prose. Oral texts are intended to travel from someone's mouth to someone else's ears. Given this purpose, song-texts are created with a view to sounding good, sounding effective and sometimes sounding beautiful. Their most obvious play on the phonic nature of language is rhyme, yet it is far from the only one. Many song-texts include repetition of vowel-sounds, and some use rhetorical techniques like onomatopoeia, alliteration and partial rhyme – phonic figures of style.

Besides, they frequently use repetition – this is both a phonic and a semantic technique, since repetition reinforces or even modifies meaning. Many song-texts have repeated sections, usually an unchanging refrain after each verse, as in "Ding Dong! Merrily". And most of the others are made up of several verses (sometimes called strophes or stanzas) often four or five lines long, which means that even without precise verbal repetition they present a periodicity of equal-sized units.

This enables each verse to be sung to the same music. A song that divides into these equal units is called "strophic", and strophic forms are especially common in popular songs, where the same music can be recycled many times, over ever-changing words. And the lines too may have a periodicity of metre (e.g. 10 syllables per line), which of course coincides with a musical phrase.

It is common for folksy texts like "Die Lorelei" (Figure 2.1) to be divided into verses ("strophes") of four or eight lines, and for the music written for the first section to do service for the others, even though the mood of the words may be different. Thus there is no verbal phrase with its own exclusive music – and the setting is called strophic. Note the occasional slurring of two notes to form a melisma. The first complete measure has words varying from 4 to 6 syllables, and so the composer Silcher calls for melismas on the syllables "schön", "Jung" and "klein".

A later composer, Liszt, took the same poem and made a through-composed setting, one where every word has music of its own. It fills more than five pages with over 100 measures, in which there is very little repetition. Whereas Silcher's song takes three minutes to sing, Liszt's takes more than twice as long (you might contrast Richard Tauber's performance on YouTube with Kiri Te Kanawa's). Choosing this "through-composed" option gave Liszt the opportunity to make variations in mood, volume, tempo (i.e. speed) and even metre. Whereas Silcher's piece sounds like a good folksong, Liszt brought more of the drama of the text into the music, with the climax marked *molto agitato* (very agitated), with the voice line rising to a high B ♭ and with fortissimo tremulos in the piano part.

The rhythmic poem-translation printed below, a nineteenth-century one by James Thomson, could easily be made to fit Silcher's strophic version but would require revision or rewriting before it could fit Liszt's.

THE LORELEY

I know not what evil is coming,
But my heart feels sad and cold:
A song in my head keeps humming,
A tale from the times of old.
The air is fresh and it darkles,
And smoothly flows the Rhine;
The peak of the mountain sparkles
In the fading sunset-shine.

The loveliest wonderful maiden
On high is sitting there,
With golden jewels braiden,
And she combs her golden hair.

With a golden comb sits combing,
And ever the while sings she

(Poem continues on p. 25.)

Figure 2.1 Die Lorelei, with discussion

This German song is so famous that the Nazis tried without success to stop people singing it. So they attributed the words to "poet unknown" . . . all because they had been written in 1822 by a Jew, the great Heinrich Heine.

This piano score can print the whole song on a single page, because the strophic setting, by Friedrich Silcher, fits the first 8 lines of text into 16 measures of music, and those 16 measures are then used twice more for the whole 24-line poem. In strophic songs the music is multi-purpose: the same tune serves for two or more sets of words. Musically the verses have the same melody and harmonies, and differ in only small ways – a bit faster or slower, a bit louder or softer.

A marvellous song through the gloaming
Of magical melody.

It hath caught the boatman and bound him
In the spell of a wild sad love;
He sees not the rocks around him,
He sees only her above.
The waves through the pass keep swinging,
But boatman or boat is none;
And this with her mighty singing
The Loreley hath done.

Song-texts are presented to audiences differently from other oral texts like speeches or even recited poetry. In performance the syllables may vary greatly in pitch and length, especially when important words have long open vowels. One syllable may be sounded very high or very low, and may even leap up or down. One syllable may take over five seconds to sing, and the music may impose rhythms quite unlike the ordinary spoken rhythms of the words – the rhythms may be jerkier, or may be weirdly uniform.

Besides, characteristic song-lyrics are often very short, with or without the repetitions. They often consist of short lines, even short phrases. The best are marvels of grace and concision. It is not uncommon to find incomplete sentences. Conversely, one rarely finds long or complex sentences – a sentence of twenty words is quick to read in print, but musical setting tends to stretch it out to 30 seconds or more.

As a good translation textbook puts it: "an effective oral text avoids the problems of comprehension arising from informational overloading, elaborate cross-reference, excessive speed and so forth" (Hervey & Higgins 1992: 136). With a written text it is usually possible to read slowly, taking cues from punctuation marks, and to re-read if necessary. Note also that oral texts cannot use spelling to distinguish between homophones – whether the English word is "sun" or "son", for example, or "sight", "site" or "cite".

The oral nature of songs also means that their language is often informal and colloquial, sometimes nonsensical and sometimes vulgar. This is especially true of songs that target a wide popular audience. Yet even here we can find that into a generally natural text a songwriter has inserted some stylised elements or some uncommon vocabulary (words that rhyme or sound good, like "thrice" or "melliferous").

The inner nature of song-lyrics

Despite the diversity of the genre, one can propose a few generalisations about the inner nature of good song-lyrics.

Emotion is a common feature. Song-lyrics are expressive texts channelling feelings such as joy and despair on subjects like love or death. Songs are seldom dominated by statements or arguments or the conveying of factual information. Colloquial language is well suited to this emotional purpose, and everyday idioms are common.

The language of songs is not objective. Often there is first-person speech ("I/me/my"), sometimes including autobiographical details or disclosures. Almost as often there are second-person addresses, typically to a singular "you". Often there are exclamations. Often there are questions, and often there are imperatives – these are forms of utterance that attract attention and seem to request a response.

And often there is drama. The "speaker" of a song may be a fictional character haranguing another, perhaps in dialectal language. One even encounters dialogue songs, which are performed by two singers (or occasionally just one acting as both characters). This resemblance of song-texts to drama-texts is of course crucial in music-theatre and opera. Less frequent – but common enough – are prominent humorous elements or narrative elements.

Many song-texts contain some of the subtleties typical of poetry. Though seldom approaching the subtlest of lyrical expression, they certainly produce resonant lines of genuine poetic strength: raw utterances of the heart's pain rescued from the pitfalls of cliché by the songwriter's verbal skill and enhanced by the magic of music. Good song-lyrics usually exploit emotionally charged words such as basic verbs (go, fall, follow, cry, dream), basic adjectives (blue, bright, sad, little) and basic nouns (fear, joy, moon, sea, eyes). These words often feature in short and effective metaphors. To translate this kind of poetic language requires sensitivity, though less skill than is needed for complex poetry. Only a minority of songs draw on obscure or archaic language, or invent new words and expressions.

Problems of sense

The term "Sense" is used here to denote the semantic matters that dominate discussions of non-fiction translating: *meaning, content and intent*. These matters are not as central with song-lyrics and are relatively less important in singable translations; but a written TT has above all the role of conveying a song's verbal meaning. We can say that Sense is badly handled whenever a TT acquires a different propositional meaning from the ST. Teachers usually evaluate translation exercises by this criterion, noting minor and major errors, and penalising students for omissions, distortions and additions to the ST meaning. With songs, the duty to preserve Sense is greatest when the ST merits particular respect, perhaps because of its poetic quality or because the value of the original song rests heavily on it.

Translation students often make the remark that: "I thought I understood this text until I began to translate it." This experience is common because the partial understanding one gains on first reading is not good enough for translators. Sometimes an apparently simple text becomes more difficult when you look closer: you merely thought you had grasped it. If a song repeats the phrase "Babies suck", you may eventually see that it is both a factual statement and a value-judgement.

Consider the old line: "Drink to me only with thine eyes" (Ben Jonson). Does the "only" mean "not to anyone else", "not with your lips"? Or perhaps "If you just drink to me . . ."? And how can you be sure? You may even consider it truly ambiguous – but the task of translating will probably force you to come off the fence. Even when you desire to retain it, the TL may not offer a way of doing so.

What exactly do these titles mean?

Bag Full of Silly	A Hard Day's Night
Positively 4th Street	The Crunge
Lay Up Under Me	Boog it!
The Flat Foot Floogie	Koala Sprint
When Daisies Pied	All We like Sheep
Waif Me	Munted

What exactly do these phrases mean?

"the child that's got his own"
"the days of Auld Lang Syne"
"when you were a camel"
"the hissing of summer lawns"
"let's get into animal"

And what about these weird collocations – verbal juxtapositions first made, perhaps, in song-lyrics: "nowhere man" . . . "material girl" . . . "hollow meadow"?

You need to really understand the ST. To translate the Australian song "Kookaburra sits in the old gum-tree", you absolutely must know that this bird makes a sort of laughing noise – that is a key detail. You also need to know that "bush" doesn't mean shrub, and that "gay" doesn't mean homosexual. But it is less important to know exactly what a gum-tree looks like (this is not a botany textbook). Indeed, one of the things you need to understand is *which of the details are less important* – because those inessential details provide locations for flexibility.

Puzzlement and misunderstanding is particularly common in foreign songs. A tourist in Paris may gasp at a Frenchman singing about bakers "making bastards", until somebody explains that *un bâtard* is a kind of loaf. A case in German is "Sapphische Ode", the title of a well-known song of Brahms. Since it clearly says "Sapphic Ode", one might think it has something to do with lesbianism. Many Germans don't know, and most translators have failed to help, held back by a narrow view of translating as a linguistic matter. A wider view would see the song-translator as a language consultant for musicians and audiences. This would produce a different outcome and should result in calling it "Ode in Sapphic Metre".

Easy to Understand?

The following song can often be heard at English sportsgrounds, sung by people who don't know (or don't care) that it is a nineteenth-century African-American song based on a passage in the Old Testament:

> *Swing low, sweet chariot,*
> *Comin' for to carry me home . . .*
> *I looked over Jordan and what did I see . . .*
> *A band of angels comin' after me . . .*

Is "swing" a noun or a verb? How can a chariot be "sweet"? Does the non-standard phrase "for to" mean "in order to"? Where is "home"? Would that be Michael Jordan? Did he drive a Mitsubishi Chariot? What kind of angels might one see at an English stadium?

Few sports fans would have all the answers, and that doesn't matter; but a translator needs to know them.

Another case would be offering the phrase "green suit" as a translation for the *habit vert* found in a song by Moustaki. That version would be inadequate: for the original audience it denoted the regalia of the French Academy. Similarly, if you lazily rendered the title "G.I. Blues" as *Le blues du G.I.*, you would be selling the reader short. The first audiences in 1960 knew that the acronym stood for General Infantryman, and that Elvis Presley was doing military service. But your audience doesn't: you should therefore help them to understand, if only by a title like *Blues du service militaire.* This is sometimes termed "explicitation": making clear some detail that was present in the ST but not explicit.

Problems of non-standard language (dialect, sociolect, slang, colloquialisms)

Normally one translates between standard forms of two languages. Yet many oral texts, naturally including songs, have non-standard features like slang or popular syntax or dialectal vocabulary. These present more problems than accent, which is merely phonetic variation from the standard. Songwriters often favour the spoken language of the street, the market or the soap opera. It can be punchy, it can be homely. For many rap and hip-hop groups, the use of standard language would be unnatural and untrue to their ghetto situation and their anti-establishment values.

What if a sentence says "nowt" instead of "nothing"? What if a sentence says "rattle yer dags, gal" or "I loves you", or "It's a great day tomorrow", or even "Is you is you is you ain't my baby?" These are not ignorant errors but deliberate deviations. Most of the jazz poets, for example, knew what standard phraseology was (that "I ain't done nothin' never" means "I didn't ever do anything") and chose to reject it.

We have to understand the phrase in context and know why the non-standard features are present – or, to state this more pointedly, know what would be lost if they were removed. And then what do we do? We choose some option appropriate to our readers, considering that here (if not elsewhere) the use of non-standard TL might be justified. What would be best for "I can't get nowhere with you"?

One corpus of non-standard song-lyrics uses African-American English: blues, jazz, gospel. That is related particularly to social class. Other non-standard songs are regional, for example Scottish songs that quote or allude to Robbie Burns:

> Leeze me on thy bonnie craigie!
> An thou live, thou'll steal a naigie . . .

This use of regional dialect is common in many languages: Italian popular songs, for example, are quite likely to use Venetian, Neapolitan or Sicilian varieties.

Slang words and expressions are natural features of songwriting, since they impart vigour and colour to the language. To translate them, you should not choose words typical of the formal written language, but opt for slangy or at least colloquial expressions in the TL.

Referring to a different type of oral text – a play-script – Newmark gave this advice, which could be applied to songs: "The important thing is to produce naturally slangy, possibly classless speech in moderation, hinting at the dialect, 'processing' only a small proportion of the SL dialect words" (1988: 195). Although that means creating a TT that is closer to the standard language than the ST was, it certainly doesn't mean totally ignoring its dialectal or sociolectal character. (For some audiences, actually, a bolder use of TL dialect might work well – moderation is not always a virtue.)

Consider the colloquial line: "He did them all in." Speakers of English as a second language may not immediately grasp that this means he killed them. But even after they do, they may still struggle to get the same colloquial effect. The phrase *Los ha matado a todos* is standard Spanish, neutral in register. But it fails to carry the same tone, and so a more slangy verb must be found.

One writer who didn't like translators to standardise his style was Mark Twain, who complained in 1875 about a French version of his comic story about a frog. The charm of the piece derived largely from the dialectal English used, yet the TT was in polished standard French. Twain commented: "He has not translated it at all; he has simply mixed it all up; it is no more like the Jumping Frog when he gets through with it than I am like a meridian of longitude . . ." This translator, he said, "can't see why it would ever convulse any one with laughter" (1977: 412). Non-standard language, when found in stories or song lyrics, is present for a reason.

Cultural issues

Verbal allusions are hard to deal with. It may happen, if the SL is not your mother tongue, that you totally fail to notice a cultural allusion in a song. You probably know what lies behind the titles "Gatman and Robbin" or "Doctor

Jekyll". But what about "The Ghost of Tom Joad"? Few could list all the pop-culture references in "American Pie"! And consider these words from the "Avocado Song":

> What can compare with this golden pear
> from the gardens of Eldorado?
> Its flesh maybe green but it's fit for a queen.
> And I'm an aficionado.

To an English-speaker this echoes a well-known nursery rhyme about a golden pear growing on a little nutty tree.

Such verbal allusions are not uncommon, drawing on a supposed store of common phrases. It may be line from a film or TV show, from a once-famous poet or politician, from a well-known folktale (e.g. "What big teeth you have!"). Sometimes allusions are confusingly brief and fragmentary: the phrase "Hell hath no fury . . ." is a truncated version of a line from Congreve: "Hell hath no fury like a woman scorned." A French translator has commented on allusions in Swedish and German songs. He explains that the line "Give us the Pentecost egg!" alludes to an old German tradition, and goes on to say that: "In France the old gods of Scandinavia and Germany are less known than those of the Greeks and Romans" (Mathé 2015). A translator should offer an explanatory note, if the context of the translation permits that.

Parody songs absolutely depend on allusion to earlier texts. A spoof hardly works at all unless the audiences know what is being spoofed. The title "The Worst Noel" makes obvious sense if you have heard a lot of English Christmas carols. But not otherwise (was it someone called Noel?).

Also quite common are musical allusions, where a snatch of melody is stolen from a well-known work. At the end of Schumann's "Widmung", for example, the piano quotes the start of Schubert's "Ave Maria", a melodic phrase that was then well known. And sometimes these kinds of allusion combine, as in the "Dance of the DNA":

> The thymine connects to the adenine
> and the cytosine to the guanine
> so that purine and pyrimidine stay equal all the way.
> And when the bases change their places
> they pick out partners to fill the spaces.
> That's how the system replicates and survives another day.

Given that this section of the song steals the tune of "Dem Bones, Dem Bones" – and even borrows three words "connects to the" – we have something culturally complex: a song based on a scientific paper in *Nature* (1953) linked to an African-American spiritual inspired by the dream of an ancient Hebrew prophet.

Such cultural issues occur more often in texts from past centuries. Your first step is to really understand; your second is to devise a bridging TT that can carry the important content to your target audience of today. You may find a need to reduce the historical content, but it would be a pity to erase it all.

Some other problems, in alphabetical order

This section will focus on specific verbal problems found more often in songs than in other texts for translation. And it will make some suggestions about how to handle these when translating. It ignores a number of annoying problems that are less present in songs (misprints, jargon, acronyms, lexical gaps, unavailable constructions) or are less serious in this genre, such as factual errors.

The approach here is not to proclaim strict guidelines, but to ask intelligent questions and to point to a wide range of "tools" that can prove useful. The best choice of tools will depend not only on the ST but also on the *skopos* . . . or as Paul Kussmaul has put it: "in each individual case we have to take text-function and target-culture into account" (1995: 69). Here are two questions about text-function: "What is that phrase doing in the text?" and "Why did the author include it?" Here are two questions about text-culture: "What did it mean to the target audience of the ST?" and "Can it mean the same in the TL?"

Supposing you find in a song a problematic word or phrase that you seldom see in print, perhaps a slang word. You need to figure out answers to several questions (not just the first):

- What does it mean?
- Why was it put there?
- What effect might it have on listeners?
- What would be lost if it were removed?

Ideally you should be able to answer all of these before you generate some TL options, the best of which, ideally, should respect the integrity of the ST and help your TT to do its job well. That advice can be applied to any particular translation problem.

Ambiguity

If a line of text seems ambiguous, is it really? What are the two meanings, and which one was intended? Try to see whether the context answers those questions. Then make a decision – you should not sit on the fence unless you are sure the ambiguity is deliberate.

Archaisms, outdated language

True archaisms, i.e. phrases that had ceased to be current before the ST was written, are not often found in song-texts. Therefore one should avoid archaisms in song-translations – even though English translators used to indulge in "thou/thee/ thine" etc. Yet many poetic texts (e.g. Metastasio's Italian libretti) used not the most common language of their day but a formal, heightened, "literary language". An appropriate TT will need to reflect that, avoiding the excesses of the pseudo-poetic, yet using words that are formal or neutral (and never too recent). There are tools for assessing when words and expressions were current: in English there is for example https://books.google.com/ngrams.

Euphemism and indirect language

With euphemism, two things are happening: on the surface polite acceptable words are being used, while underneath them lies something "not so nice". For example the English phrase "the other place" can denote Hell, and the name "Davy Jones" can signify drowning. The French word for "disappearance" some-times means death. Such euphemisms can be difficult, because first you need to grasp what is really being said, and then you must try to convey that underlying meaning in a way that's neither too direct nor too indirect. If the target audi-ence is left wondering "Is that some Welshman?", then the meaning has not been transferred. There is a song which says "You'd lost your taste for water", where the context identifies the hidden message as "You started to hit the booze". The ideal translation would have to make that message apparent, and yet convey it by indirect means, as the ST did.

Fixed expressions

All languages have their idioms, clichés, proverbs and other fixed expressions. Some of these are arbitrary and puzzling (e.g. the English "by and large"). Trans-lation textbooks give general advice on recognising and handling these idioms, for example Mona Baker's (1992/2011) *In Other Words*. Normally one translates the meaning and not the wording: only in English can it "rain cats and dogs." A complicating factor is that some songwriters (and other wordsmiths) manipu-late existing fixed phrases. What if the phrase "barking up the wrong tree" (mean-ing off-target) occurred in a song about forest protection? What if the phrase "bat out of hell" was used in relation to real bats? What if a Canadian song said: "it was raining cats and raccoons"? With such phrases, you will need to apply your own lateral thinking – Google Translate will not help!

Foreign phrases

It can happen that a song in one language contains some words or phrases in another (a Swedish lyric with some English, a German one with some Latin etc.). The upstream questions are: "What are those foreign elements doing there? Why did the lyricist insert them? Was it for rhyme, for stylistic effect, for precision of sense or what?" How you answer those questions will help you choose between the options available to you, as will the downstream question of what your audi-ence will best appreciate. A good rule of thumb is that "whether a third-language word in a text is transferred or translated depends on whether it is used for 'expres-sive' or 'informative' purposes" (Newmark 1988: 182).

Incomplete sentences

These are more common in songs and dramatic texts than in prose. But do not assume that they are equally common in all languages. If your TL tolerates incompleteness less than the SL, you may wish to "correct" it for the sake of a more coherent text. But not otherwise.

Irony

An English line such as "Goodness gracious, how audacious!" is probably ironic. Not only is "audacious" a high-register word of Latin origin, it is often spoken with eyebrows raised. This irony may need further signalling in a Romance language where the cognate words are unmarked everyday words. Verbal irony can be hard to identify, because it lies more in the tone than the words. Translators may need to make this tone clearer. Possible tactics include:

(a) blatant irony, reducing the subtlety
(b) a question expressing doubt
(c) a straight negative.

Thus if you know that a phrase like "Nobody buys sushi" is intended ironically, you might consider options such as

(a) No one ever buys sushi!
(b) Does anyone buy sushi?
(c) Sushi sells very well!

Humour, jokes, puns

If a song is particularly rich in jokes and "laugh lines", you should think about what exactly makes them funny. The two difficult kinds of humour, for translators, are language-specific and culture-specific. Fortunately there are many other kinds: humour based on understatement, paradox, absurdity, discrepancy, playfulness, bathos, juxtaposition, sudden switching, amusing irony, unexpected crudeness, or shameless audacity. Even when verbally expressed, these are not wordplay, and so they should prove very translatable, provided you go for similar effect rather than identical wording.

With language-specific humour, notably puns, you may need to step back from the detail and create a new pun in the TL or use a different humorous device that has the same general humorous intention. Sometimes it is easier to translate a comic text when you don't get all the jokes! It is even permissible, when laughter is required by the *skopos*, to call on some verbal techniques not found in the ST – for example to resort to coinage or comic mispronunciation. In the case of puns, here are three possibilities:

• *Create a new pun* connected verbally with the ST, thus achieving a kind of dynamic equivalence.

- *Use a different humorous device*, particularly where the humour is more important than the meaning.
- *Use compensation in place*, to ensure there is some wordplay present somewhere near the pun.

As for culture-specific humour, such as allusion, you have to find an option that communicates with the audience. Here the problematic phrase may need to be adapted freely, and there is a strong case of domestication – reference to a person or place in the target culture.

Some people think that translating humour requires sheer luck or brilliance. But a more optimistic view shows that analysis and technique can help and assumes that translators are clever enough to use and develop the skills to supplement a step-by-step approach to problems with the creative and indirect methods of lateral thinking. Some useful tips are given in "Translating Jokes and Puns" (Low 2011).

Metaphor and simile

Song lyrics are often rich in metaphor. "You are my sunshine", said an old serenade. "I am a rock", sings Paul Simon. We know not to take such lines literally. "My love is a red, red rose", said an old song of Burns, who was actually thinking of a bonny lassie. The French song which begins "Mon enfant, ma sœur" does not literally address either child or sister. And the jazz classic "Stormy weather" is not really about meteorology – a translator who fails to realise this might produce a phrase that's more about isobars than emotion.

It is important to notice metaphor. Fortunately, metaphors in song tend to be uncomplicated: readily comprehensible and seldom extended across many lines as can happen in poems. It is a good idea to pause and think what kinds of metaphor a songwriter is using – so as to sense better what is happening in the words, and then to decide how to handle them in translating. Was that a dead metaphor, a cliché metaphor, a stock metaphor, an adapted metaphor, a recent metaphor or an original metaphor? These types of metaphor are all discussed by authorities on translation (for example Newmark 1988). But is not always easy, in your second or third language, to judge whether the metaphor is unimportant (e.g. a cliché) or whether its sheer novelty delighted the ears of its first audience. How should one approach Dylan's line about "men with their hammers bleeding"? Or the Beatles' line about "her face that she keeps in a jar by the door?"

In normal translating one often reduces a metaphor into literal language: "Kill two birds with one stone" may become "Solve two problems at once." But given the poetic or semi-poetic nature of song-texts, translators should attempt to maintain the richness of metaphor, especially when it contributes to the beauty, gusto or humour of a lyric. This may at times mean replacing a metaphor about birds with one about farm animals that fits the needs of the song. It may even mean introducing metaphor in a place where the ST was literal, to compensate for loss of richness elsewhere.

Related to metaphor is the device called "simile": for example "like a diamond in the sky". Songs have used simile since before the time of Solomon. Simile can be viewed as a subset of metaphor: it is a metaphor which signals its linking nature through explicit words such as "like" or "as". You may at times add such signalling words when transferring a metaphor (thus clarifying the comparison) or conversely "translate them by omission", turning a simile into a straight metaphor.

Neologisms (new words and coined phrases)

It is not surprising that some songs contain neologisms: words and phrases coined as part of the songwriters' conscious play with language. Usually these are easy to understand, since most new words and phrases are adapted from old ones: they are derived words, novel collocations, or old words used in new senses. They can be motivated by meaning, rhythm or sound, and this will usually be apparent. If they are humorous, then the transgressive element of the coinage (disobeying the dictionary!) is part of the humour – and you should try to replicate it.

A good frame of reference for neologisms is given by Newmark, who insists that in expressive texts you are entitled to create a neologism or introduce a foreign word into your TT (1988: 150). Thus for any Spanish version of *Mary Poppins* one should certainly coin the word *supercalifragilisticoespialidoso* – and the translator probably did. It is true that some languages are more tolerant of neologisms than others. But songwriters, as creative wordsmiths, have a licence to annoy the pedantic "legislators of words", and so do song-translators!

Repetition

Repetition is found in many song-texts, often matching the repetition that is even more widespread in music. A common formula for songs is several verses (all different) each followed by a refrain (unchanging). This makes particularly good sense when a solo singer performs the verses and the audience sings along in the refrain – "the chorus".

Translators should devote special attention to repeated lines of text. Work hard to find the best option! And here's a thought: the same line or phrase does not have to be translated the same way every time. For example instead of saying "There is no other path, there is no other path", your TT could be "There is no other path, this is the only path."

Rhyme

Rhyme is a strong characteristic of songs: in many languages many songs rhyme, even in languages where most poetry doesn't rhyme (e.g. twenty-first-century English). One question to ask about a rhyming song is: "Are the rhymes central to the conception of this song, or have they been included merely out of convention?" Another useful question – if the ST wording has something strange about it – is: "Are those two words present only because of their rhyming sound, or do they actually contribute to meaning?" The phrase "I have tears in my ears" may have been chosen for its sound not its meaning. The French number *cent vingt* may have been chosen in a song because it offers an easy rhyme – unlike 120 in English – and if so, it might be fine to translate it as "99".

A large section of chapter 6 is devoted to rhyme in the TT: Do you want rhyme? What quantity? What quality?

Vulgarity and obscenity

Vulgar language is common in some genres of song, notably in rap, which seems to observe no taboo on "four-letter words". We know, most of us, that notions of obscene language and taboo words differ greatly from place to place and vary over time, because they are constructed culturally, not naturally.

So if you encounter a vulgar phrase or a case of "hate speech", ask yourself what its motivation or purpose was: did it merely express strong feeling, or was it actually intended to give offence? Decisions around obscenity require a translator to know both cultures well, and to focus not on the literal terminology of sex, excretion or blasphemy, but on the levels of offensiveness. How many people were really offended by "Just don't give a f – k"? One danger is to turn a fairly mild vulgarity in the ST into something very vile in the TT. This can happen with the French songwriter Brassens – according to Joe Flood: "To an American listener, the repetition of the f word makes Brassens out to be a loud-mouth boor, not the nuanced poet of the vernacular that he was." "His gallicisms [. . .] do not sound as harsh to French ears as their equivalents do to English, especially American, ears" (2015).

But the converse danger is excessive caution: *risqué* jokes need to remain *risqué*, and genuinely foul insults need to retain the power to offend, because otherwise the TT is less realistic and less dramatic than it should be. Vulgar language is not uncommon in film dialogue, and a book about subtitling gives this advice: "One difficulty in translating such words is to determine exactly where they range on the scale of rudeness" . . . "Floods of obscenities should be toned down . . . but it is not the subtitler's task to act as a censor (unless it is explicitly required by the client)" (Ivarsson & Carroll 1998: 126–127).

Quite right: censorship is not part of the translator's job: we try to replicate, not eviscerate. When someone who works as a translator makes deliberate choices to "tone down" vulgar language, then that person is acting (justifiably or not) as a censor, editor or adaptor and not as a translator. A translator who is too genteel to ever use words that could give offence is in the wrong profession!

The specifics of the source language

Every language has peculiarities. As a result, one should be especially aware of the habits of the SL you are dealing with. For example if it regularly names the object owned before the owner (as in *la casa de Juanita*), then that word-order is not significant: English and German can choose to name the owner first, but Spanish cannot. Furthermore, it is likely that every language-pair has particular problems, which emerge in the translating process. For example languages which do not constantly distinguish singular from plural (such as Chinese) create dilemmas when the TL is one that does.

Some features of English

Many users of this book will wish to translate out of English. This language has millions of speakers, of course, using several major varieties (British, US, Indian) and dozens of sub-varieties. It is worth noting here some of its features which may give problems – and some which you could not normally expect to replicate in another language.

- English has a huge store of words, a mongrel lexicon containing many synonyms – notably where words of Latin origin exist alongside Anglo-Saxon words (e.g. liberty/freedom, pardon/forgive, menace/threaten).
- English has many short uninflected words, notably monosyllabic verbs which can also function as nouns.
- English likes to place nouns side by side – collocate them – so that the first somehow characterises the second (e.g. baby powder, custard powder, powder room).
- English has over a hundred phrasal verbs (e.g. to come/go/run + round/with/over/up with). In most cases a short everyday verb is followed by a kind of preposition, which greatly alters the meaning. The register tends to be colloquial.
- English has a fairly rigid word-order: for example adjectives precede nouns, something that many languages find illogical.
- English uses numerous affixes – prefixes and suffixes – and permits innovative manipulation of many of these.
- English often introduces relative clauses without the pronouns "that" and "which" (these are optional, even in written English).
- English has a system of spelling that is confused in itself and confusing to everyone!

One general difficulty may be the range of near-synonyms in English, exceeding most other languages (does any other language even have a thesaurus?). Nuances can easily be lost. And yet ambiguities are quite common, whether deliberate or unintentional. Another issue is the relative concision of English, notably its short punchy verbs – many other languages require more syllables to say the same thing. This may be a reason for you to under-translate, to omit some of the details, especially if your song-translation needs to economise on syllables. So you have to judge which details are less important.

Untranslatable songs?

This chapter has mentioned a large number of "upstream issues": problems located in the STs themselves. This may prompt the question of whether some songs can be declared untranslatable.

It is likely that some songs – a small minority – are impossible to translate at all well, for reasons that are linguistic, cultural or both. Nevertheless, you should beware of the word "impossible". Not even the "two-hour marathon" is impossible! (Admittedly, many athletes have tried it without success; yet anyone who declares it impossible today would be silly now and will surely be proved wrong before 2050.)

Douglas Hofstadter's book about literary translation has this to say: "When something is said to be 'untranslatable', be skeptical. What this claim often means is that it would be impossible *for a dullard* to translate the work in question: that it takes some *thought* and *intelligence* to recreate it in another language. In short, *to translate something witty requires a witty translator.* This is hardly profound, and yet witty translators don't seem to be in the mind of people who prematurely pronounce so many works 'untranslatable'" (1997: 394, *his emphasis*).

Hofstadter notes a particular work that had been claimed to be untranslatable – the witty verse found in Christian Morgenstern's *Galgenlieder* – and then says that this claim has been disproved, by the translator Max Knight. He might have added that the profession which produces simultaneous interpreters should surely be capable of doing ten impossible things before breakfast.

But a few songs do pose too many problems, and a combination of cultural and linguistic ones must be the worst. For example Pierre Perret's song "Bercy Madeleine" names some eighty stations on the Paris Métro (cultural information) and uses dozens of those names to make puns (linguistic acrobatics). This could not really be translated. And yet one can imagine it inspiring a virtuoso song that made puns on the names of dozens of stations on the New York subway. This would be classifiable as an adaptation (see chapter 7).

***

Exercise (A)

Here is a lyric by Shakespeare. It comes from the distant past, yet it is sung whenever *The Tempest* is performed:

> Where the bee sucks, there suck I;
> In a cowslip's bell I lie;
> There I couch when owls do cry.
> On the bat's back I do fly
> After summer merrily.
> Merrily, merrily shall I live now
> Under the blossom that hangs on the bough.

Identify what upstream problems it would pose for a translator, explain exactly why they are problematic, and say how you might approach the task of solving them.

Exercise (B)

Invent four lines of a lyric, in your home language, which would be very hard to translate on account of language-specific elements, and culture-specific elements also. Then challenge other students to translate them – or at least to discuss the nature of the difficulties.

Further reading

This chapter covers matters discussed in many translation courses. It has referenced three major textbooks in particular:

Baker, Mona (1992 & 2011) *In Other Words*, London & New York, Routledge. This deals well with many issues, for example idioms and fixed expressions.

Hervey, S. & Higgins, I. (1992) *Thinking Translation*, London & New York, Routledge. (Hervey and/or Higgins collaborated on several sequels to this textbook, focusing on French, German, Spanish, Italian and Arabic.)

Newmark, Peter (1988) *A Textbook of Translation*, New York, Prentice Hall. This gives very good tips on a wide range of tricky matters, including metaphors, clichés and jargon.

References

Aue, Walter (2015, August 22) Personal communication.

Baker, Mona (1992 & 2011) *In Other Words*, London & New York, Routledge.

Flood, Joe (2015, November 13) Personal communication.

Hofstadter, Douglas (1997) *Le ton beau de Marot, in Praise of the Music of Language*, New York, Basic Books.

Ivarsson, Jan & Carroll, Mary (1998) *Subtitling*, Simrishamn, Transedit.

Kussmaul, Paul (1995) *Training the Translator*, Philadelphia, Benjamins.

Lerner, A. J. (1978) *The Street Where I Live*, London, Hodder & Stoughton.

Low, Peter (2011) "Translating Jokes and Puns" in *Perspectives* 19/1, 59–70.

Mathé, Pierre (2015, August 28) Personal communication.

Minors, Helen (ed) (2012) *Music, Text and Translation*, London, Bloomsbury.

Newmark, Peter (1988) *A Textbook of Translation*, New York, Prentice Hall.

Newmark, Peter (2012) "Art Song in Translation", in Minors, H. (ed) *Music, Text and Translation*, London, Bloomsbury.

Reiss, Katharina (1971/2001) *Translation Criticism, Potential and Limitations,* Manchester, St Jerome.

Twain, Mark (1977) *The Comic Mark Twain Reader*, ed. Charles Neider, New York, Doubleday.

3   Translations to read

Or to otherwise accompany the performance of songs in the SL

When a song will be performed in a language unfamiliar to most of the audience, some kind of translating must occur, because otherwise the verbal elements of the song will be lost. They may not be totally lost, since a good performance can communicate something of the song's mood, but they will be largely lost: those who say: "I don't understand Spanish, but I understood that song" are mistaken. Mere sounds without meanings can even mislead, as with the pretty-sounding word "melanoma".

How can translators help to meet the needs of audiences? How can we help the singers and other musicians to present the vocal works? If we fail to think carefully about this question, then our work will be sub-optimal.

Suppose a singer or choir-director comes to you saying: "We're performing this song in Polish, and we need to give the audience the translation." A strong response would be: "Which translation? You seem to assume that there exists one all-purpose translation, but that assumption is false." A milder response might be more tactful, yet should elicit the information you need for your task, information about purpose – notably whether the translation will be printed, screened or spoken.

The Greek word for goal or purpose is *skopos*, and it is widely used in translation theory, particularly by "functionalist" scholars such as Hans J. Vermeer, for whom the term designates the "goal or purpose, defined by the commission and if necessary adjusted by the translator" (1989: 230). Could this apply to songs? It certainly applies to advertising jingles, which are short songs commissioned by the people who pay for them, who define their purpose as persuasion: the selling of products. This obvious functionality is quite untypical of songs, whose words are normally expressive; yet Vermeer's definition draws attention usefully to stakeholders other than the author: the translator who may indeed want the right to "adjust", and the end-users – the many people for whom the translation is made. When assessing a TT, according to "Skopos Theory" "the standard will not be intertextual coherence but adequacy or appropriateness with regard to the *skopos*" (Nord 1997: 33). In recent decades such functionalist thinking has proved a useful counterweight to earlier views of translating which focused on ST and author. It has been applied particularly to informative and persuasive texts; but it has some relevance to literary texts also. Some song-lyrics have at least an ostensible purpose – lullabies to soothe, serenades to court – and many singers create or choose songs with the conscious intention of charming, inspiring or amusing their audiences.

This book was prompted, in part, by the existence of bad translations – bad in the sense of not being fit-for-purpose. Before the late twentieth century many people viewed translating as a purely linguistic exercise, one of creating a TT to match a ST. They would think that a line from *Carmen* should be "correctly" translated as

The brass rods of the sistra would ring with a metallic jangle

Yet this is a folksy Gipsy song, no place for an obscure technical word like "sistra". Most of the purposes for which one might translate that song dictate a different choice, one more suited to the needs of the audience.

The present chapter is unashamedly functionalist. It seeks to encourage thinking about the *skopos* of a song-translation. It focuses particularly on the many cases where there is a change of medium: the ST is an oral text for singing, but the TT will not be sung, and so the translator must change a ST in one medium (oral text for singing) into another medium. Where the TT is in written form, on paper or on screen, and this means that at the very least it will need to conform to the conventions of written language – notably in layout and punctuation.

Much vocal music is indeed performed in the SL, for good reasons. But too often the verbal dimension of the songs is totally ignored. On radio, for example, one may hear only the title of a foreign song, and nothing about the words – even when the musician, lyricist or performer considered the words important. Of course they often did, especially if they wrote the words themselves: think of Björk of Iceland, Brel of Belgium, Tom Jobim of Brazil.

Distinct strategies according to purpose

The present chapter explores what best practice might be for all but one of the most likely *skopoi*. The one purpose not discussed here – the "singable translation" intended for performance in the TL, in concert hall or karaoke bar – will be the focus of chapters 5 and 6.

Here is a simple chart of non-singable purposes:

Skopos	Kind of translation
1 Study	Word-for-word/Gloss
2a Printed programme	Communicative
2b CD insert	Semantic
3 Surtitles and subtitles	Communicative/Gist
4 Spoken intro	Gist

The main point of this chart is to help translators meet the various specific needs of musicians, by helping them to clarify their needs.

1 Study translations

These are of minority interest only. They are not intended for the audiences of songs!

The users requiring the best understanding of the source text are performers, choir directors or singing teachers. Usually they are working on "classical" vocal music, where one often sings in a foreign language. But American jazz classics could usefully be translated in this way for foreigners, and indeed at any time when a complex song will be sung in the SL by performers who don't know that language well. Study translations are designed to help the singers to really follow and understand how the text functions in detail, not just its general meaning. For them, according to Emily Ezust: "a poetic translation could be as unhelpful as a paraphrase – or possibly even misleading, as it might obscure or displace the particular sense of each word in the original language" (2012). A word-for-word approach is certainly useful for a study translation.

Editions of vocal music commonly print translations for the singer to study while rehearsing the song. These may appear near the start of the volume, or at the start of each song or in the end-papers. Often such translations are presented in parallel format for line-by-line comparison; sometimes the layout is interlinear, with the TT placed under the ST. (They are not, however, underlaid within the musical score, as happens with singable translations, because the song will be performed in the SL.)

In addition, there can be a place for adding explanations of linguistic or cultural details. One term that matches this kind of translation is "gloss translation". As used by Eugene Nida, this means a translation "designed to permit the reader to identify himself as fully as possible with the person in the source-language context." The translator "attempts to reproduce as literally and meaningfully as possible the form and content of the original", and even uses footnotes "in order to make the text fully comprehensible" (Nida 1964: 159).

A gloss translation in this case will enlighten singers about the "sub-textual" matters, at least when the impact of a song depends heavily on them. Because some song-lyrics use language in a very concentrated way, translators should be willing to explicate them, to show the sense of phrases, the definitions and even the connotations of words. They can and should gloss complex words, using square brackets or footnotes. This is particularly important when a phrase is opaque due of cultural specificity, historical allusion or complexity. There is even a place for "split translations" offering dual versions of a word or sentence fragment. Such gloss translations may also explain double meanings and allusions, particularly if these were well understood by the original audience.

Makers of study translations should take the time to tease out such content, so as to help the singer perform the phrase more intelligently – whereas other kinds of translation must, for pragmatic reasons, be shorter and clearer. One would not expect an ordinary translation to explain "All Souls' Day" (the title of a Strauss song), but a study translation for Chinese singers could append a note about the day of the year and its significance in European Christian culture. Similarly, in the case of the "Sapphische Ode" (mentioned in chapter 2) an informative footnote could say: "Hans Schmidt gave his lyric this title because he chose an ancient metrical pattern of syllables used by the female poet Sappho – so this was a German attempt to imitate the metres of early Greek poetry."

This kind of translation can be complex: it is meant to be read more than once. The readers may have some knowledge of the SL (Italian, for example), but they need more help, and translators with a deep view of the content of a text should provide it. According to John Glenn Paton, the author of *Foundations of Singing*: "The singer wants to know meanings, even double meanings, that will shape the interpretation" (2006). Generally speaking, a deep understanding of text results in a more expressive performance.

Yet some prose translations don't take the singers beyond the obvious. For example they might easily understand that *remis à la Saint-Glinglin* says "postponed till the feast of St Glinglin", without realising the key meaning: "postponed indefinitely, to a date that exists on no calendar". In an extreme case, the song "Le disparu" (Desnos/Poulenc, c1945) has the vague sentence *Ils l'ont amené*, which actually means "The Gestapo took him away" – that historical detail, present in the subtext, must surely affect the way the musicians perform it!

One ambitious book intended for study is *Lieder Line by Line, and Word for Word* by Lois Phillips, which first appeared in 1979. It adopts a double strategy of providing both a pedantically close version (in interlinear format, word for word) and a "clear prose version" (line by line) intended "to disentangle the often unintelligible series of words resulting from a literal word-for-word translation" (1979: vi). The former version is designed to help people to engage with the foreign words and even the word order; the latter gives a better sense of the whole poem.

Now translation students are commonly told to avoid a "word-for-word" approach. And rightly so: such an approach rules out some of the normal tools that competent translators have in their toolbox and use constantly – tools such as transposing parts of speech, changing word-order, and paraphrasing. But in the hands of Phillips, "line-by-line" produces texts which appropriately fulfil a particular purpose, namely study by singers. While her word-for-word versions are very awkward, they are sufficiently clear when studied carefully. Besides, these word-for-word versions are not expected to stand alone: thus she happily offers lines such as:

"Saw a boy a (little) rose to stand"

How can this be acceptable? It ignores naturalness, notably in word-order. Yet this version is perfect – i.e. "totally fit for purpose" – for matching Goethe's original: "Sah ein Knab' ein Röslein stehn." Of course it would be quite unfit for any other purpose, as Phillips is well aware: she knows her readers will compare it with her other version of the same line:

"A boy saw a wild rose growing"

The word-for-word translation is never adequate for poetic texts, and is acceptable only when combined with another version that reads more like real poetry. But together her two versions are very helpful to singers and other Anglophones with little sense of German. They manage to provide views of "both the trees and the forest". Thinking along the same lines John Glenn Paton has said: "my publications include the word-for-word (unreadable in English), as well as the idiomatic translation, and as well as commentary" (2013).

For a true study translation, of course, musicians ought to prefer the full sense of the text. The translator should at least offer it. The extra space available is an opportunity to elucidate facts that were implicit in the ST (e.g. the identities of people or places) – if these were known by the first audience, then they were present in the subtext! The song "À la Santé" (Apollinaire/Honegger) assumes that you know La Santé to be a Paris prison; therefore a TT for foreigners ought to spell out that fact. Similarly, double meanings can be untangled, and pronouns can be clarified, since confusion sometimes enters during the translation process, and we can't tell from the TT what the pronoun "it" refers to. Cultural details can be explained too. Even if some of these can be Googled, why not provide them along with your translation? With this *skopos*, you can ignore the usual requirement for a translation to be economical.

This possibility is not limited to classical songs. The Broadway hit "The Lady is a Tramp" could surely benefit. Which of the six meanings of "tramp" applies here? And if it's really that one, then she can't be a lady, or can she? A translator-consultant could usefully tease out the irony of the song. One might even make some comment on linguistic matters, since some readers might be interested. One might, for example, add remarks such as these:

- this phrase is ironical – the speaker is only pretending to be shocked;
- the elided word in this German sentence is *habe*;
- the pronoun translated as "you" is singular and intimate;
- the number *septante*, though non-standard, is normal in Belgian French;
- the unexpected meaning of this word derives from Cockney rhyming slang . . .

For the other *skopoi* (below), the options of footnotes or editorial brackets are either impossible or very undesirable.

Incidentally, that double provision of a word-for-word version and a clear natural version might tempt some people to devise singable versions for songs in languages that they don't know. These would exploit the linguistic skills of one person and the wordsmith skills of another. To produce the best results this method should involve real collaboration.

There might be times, also, when a translator gives a singer advice about pronunciation, even if the song can be heard on YouTube. If the ST uses another alphabet or writing system (Cyrillic, Chinese etc.), then a transcription into the International Phonetic Alphabet (IPA) could be more useful than a standard transcription. IPA is useful for languages like Polish too, because Roman script certainly does not solve pronunciation problems (not in Hungarian, Turkish, Fijian or Kiswahili . . . let alone English). Such tips on pronunciation may seem to go beyond the translator's role – until you start viewing the translator as a language consultant rather than a mere decoder of meaning.

One study translation

If a singer wanted to sing a drinking song well known in Germany, then this TT for "Altassyrisch" (see box) might be ideal. The words were written in 1854 by J. V. von Scheffel, possibly in a student tavern. A "study translation" – unlike any other kind – enables a singer to decipher the ST word-order. For this particular song it might also add footnotes about the place-names, and the stone tablets, and the likelihood that the Nubian servant had dark skin.

Altassyrisch – Ancient Assyrian [Song]

Im schwarzen Walfisch zu Askalon, da trank ein Mann drei Tag´,
In the Black Whale in Ashkelon there drank a man for three days

bis dass er steif wie ein Besenstiel am Marmortische lag.
until he stiff as a broom-handle on the marble table lay.

Im schwarzen Walfisch zu Askalon da sprach der Wirt: "Halt an!
In the Black Whale in Ashkelon there spoke the innkeeper: "Stop!

Der trinkt von meinem Dattelsaft mehr als er zahlen kann."
He's drinking of my date-juice more than he pay can."

Im schwarzen Walfisch zu Askalon da bracht´ der Kellner Schar
In the Black Whale in Ashkelon there brought the waiters' crowd

in Keilschrift auf sechs Ziegelstein´ dem Gast die Rechnung dar.
in cuneiform script on six bricks to the customer the bill.

Im schwarzen Walfisch zu Askalon da sprach der Gast "O weh!
In the Black Whale in Ashkelon there spoke the customer: "Oh woe!

Mein bares Geld ging alles drauf im Lamm zu Ninive !"
My ready money went all away in the Lamb in Niniveh!"

Im schwarzen Walfisch zu Askalon da schlug die Uhr halb vier,
In the Black Whale in Ashkelon then struck the clock half to four.

da warf der Hausknecht aus Nubierland den Fremden vor die Tür.
Then threw the servant from Nubia the foreigner out the door.

Im schwarzen Walfisch zu Askalon wird kein Prophet geehrt,
In the Black Whale in Ashkelon is no prophet honoured,

und wer vergnügt dort leben will, zahlt bar, was er verzehrt.
and whoever satisfied there to live wishes, pays cash for what he consumes.

2a Programme translations for reading in concert programmes

A different *skopos* is the TT intended for the audience to read in the concert hall. In a formal concert it is still common for a printed programme to give translations of songs not performed in the language of the audience.

A text for use in a recital or concert program needs to be reader-friendly, so that it can be digested in a relatively limited time. As John Glenn Paton puts it: "The audience at a recital wants idiomatic English, understandable at a glance" (Paton 2013). Translators should therefore reduce the processing effort required by the TT. This means natural language that is reasonably intelligible and idiomatic, as the ST usually was. It also means normal punctuation, even if the written ST was unpunctuated. It is unlikely, however, to do justice to the depth and subtlety of a poetic song-lyric.

Such translations may be printed in prose format, or as unrhymed free verse. Sometimes the ST is printed in parallel text; but even then you are free to view a whole sentence or stanza as the "unit to be translated". You should, however, maintain the larger structures of the original.

Classical singers performing to English-speaking audiences have often taken these translations from printed books, for example *The Ring of Words, an Anthology of Song Texts*, by Philip Miller (1963), *The Interpretation of French Song* by Pierre Bernac (1970), *The Fischer-Dieskau Book of Lieder* by Dietrich Fischer-Dieskau (1977), which calls itself a "reference book for the recital-goer, record-lover and musician", and *A French Song Companion* by Graham Johnson and Richard Stokes (1999). These printed books offer TTs in the form of unrhymed free verse, carefully rendered without great departures from the ST meaning. They present the meaning line by line, wherever this is reasonably possible – short lines can make it difficult – but within the lines they certainly don't favour word for word.

Nowadays performers often turn to the Internet, especially to an amazing database of song-texts and translations called the LiederNet Archive (http://www.lieder.net/)

Despite the German word *Lieder*, this website covers dozens of languages, with input from dozens of volunteer translators. Its emphasis is on Art Songs, typically works in the classical tradition for piano and voice, but includes choral works as well. It was founded in 1995 by Emily Ezust of Canada, who has this to say:

> **Translation style**. Many of the translations are close to literal and meant primarily as an aid for understanding the original language, while others attempt to capture some of the original's rhythm or rhyme. Different types of translations are useful in different situations, and a second opinion is often quite useful, so we are always happy to offer more than one translation to the same language.
>
> (Ezust 2015)

Bergamasques?

Consider the start of Paul Verlaine's "Clair de lune":

Votre âme est un paysage choisi
Que vont charmant masques et bergamasques . . .

Your soul is a chosen landscape
charmed by masquers and revellers . . .

This TT is used frequently for recital programmes, because the poem inspired musical settings by Debussy, Fauré and others. Yet it has under-translated line 2, telling us merely that the "masques et bergamasques" are people wearing masks and having fun. That TT might pass muster in a printed recital programme, for people to glance at before hearing the song in French. But a singer might (should?) want to know more, particularly about this rare word "bergamasques".

For a study translation one could add this footnote:

The term "bergamasques" here denotes Italian comedians with col-ourful costumes (originally from the town of Bergamo), notably those depicted in the paintings of Watteau. The poet Verlaine was undoubt-edly thinking of Watteau's scenes featuring lutes and statues and foun-tains. Google Watteau and look at his paintings to get a sense of the right mood and scene, particularly if you are performing Fauré's set-ting, which has a minuet rhythm reminiscent of that period (c.1700–20).

This resource is varied in style, and doubtless in quality, but singers are enthusi-astic about it, since it has helped them to understand and communicate the verbal dimension of many songs – now over 27,000 translations. The main use for its translations has probably been in concert programmes. Students of singing in the US who are preparing their junior recitals – and who need to perform in three languages – are told to consult this archive and to seek permission to print the relevant translations. But as Emily Ezust says, "different types of translations are useful in different situations." Some translations on the site are even singable in the TL – these are unlikely to be suitable for any other *skopos*. She has stressed the functional simplicity of many translations:

These days it is quite common for the translations of art song texts to dis-pense with the usual poetic attributes – that is, basically to be unostenta-tious (grammatical) prose broken up into lines, or what I like to think of as mostly-literal-but-not-glaringly-so. This is the most common type of transla-tion found on the website I run.

The goal is to help people understand the original-language text as they hear it being sung, it must be understood that this is quite a different goal from that of publishing something someone might read to oneself or recite for pleasure without immediate recourse to the original-language poem.

[A translation can be] something simple that is not intended to live an independent life as a poem in its own right, but rather to be straight-forward and clear, and help someone hearing (and, ideally, looking at) the original poem find some meaning to otherwise incomprehensible words.

(Ezust 2012)

What if the text is a real poem, a highly rated poem? Well, it is being translated not as a poem but as words allied to music. Song-translations are not stand-alone texts but adjunct texts. What will be heard is the poem as transmuted into song, and so the musicians (composer, singer, accompanist) will share with the translator the task of communicating the poem's richness and subtlety. If you regret, as some do, that no one English word conveys the subtle richness of a ST word (like the German *Sehnsucht* meaning longing, aspiration, desire, nostalgia, wistfulness, yearning . . .), then you can hope, at least, that the singer will help by a rich and subtle performance.

A comparable resource, used for more recent popular songs, is lyricstranslate. com, which publishes the work of volunteer translators in dozens of languages. The quality of work is variable, as one might expect with enthusiasts. The number of translations found here is huge: approaching 300,000. On any given day you will find new translations for songs by such performers as Madonna, Heldmaschine and Jennifer Lopez, along with "requests" for versions of songs from (perhaps) Greece and Kyrgyzstan.

Communicative or semantic?

The kind of translation recommended here as most suitable for the concert programme matches the term "communicative translation", as used by Peter Newmark. A communicative translation, by his definition, is written at the linguistic level of the intended readers, and attempts "to render the exact contextual meaning of the original in such a way that both content and language are readily acceptable and comprehensible to the readership" (1988: 47).

Now his general recommendation is that communicative translation be used for informative texts, but not for expressive texts like song-lyrics. What if the words have high poetic merit, as with a Shakespeare song – normally a literary text should not be reduced to the linguistic level of the majority. But this *skopos* is an exception: the circumstances of the concert-room mean that priority should go to the needs of the readers.

For example a famous lyric poem by Baudelaire has the lines:

Les soleils couchants
Revêtent les champs
D'hyacinthe et d'or.

and the Liedernet translation gives:

> *The westering suns*
> *clothe the fields*
> *with reddish-orange and gold.*

This tells us he is evoking sunset colours, but avoids the complication that *hyacinthe* (more often spelt *jacinthe*) is a precious stone. Such under-translation is probably better suited to a concert programme than is a more poetic line such as "with garnet and gold". Neither version does full justice to the original; yet both are good adjuncts to the wonderful song-setting by Henri Duparc.

Actually, the "garnet and gold" option may be better for a CD insert. This is a similar *skopos* to a concert programme, but not identical. With a live audience you can probably make some generalisations about their knowledge of cultural and linguistic matters. You may assess, for example, which minor details in the source text may be omitted at little cost, which cultural details may be "domesticated" into the target culture and which proper names may require some elucidation.

Here is a Spanish example, part of a folksong – anonymous, given classy music by Obradors – along with a draft translation:

> Del cabello más sutil
> Que tienes en tu trenzada
> He de hacer una cadena
> Para traerte a mi lado
> Una **alcarraza** en tu casa,
> Chiquilla, quisiera ser,
> Para besarte en la boca
> Cuando fueras a beber.

> *With the very soft hair*
> *that you have in your tresses,*
> *I would like to make a chain*
> *to use to pull you to my side.*
> *And I would like to be a jug*
> *in your house, little darling,*
> *so as to be able to kiss you*
> *whenever you take a drink.*

Consider line five. Although the *alcarraza* is a kind of jug, that normal word is problematical, because nobody drinks directly from jugs or pitchers. This Spanish vessel, however, does touch the lips of some people, notably the beloved woman in this lyric. Therefore it would be justifiable to opt for an adjacent word like "cup" – you would lose the precision of meaning, but you would also lose an unwanted distraction.

2b CD inserts and singers' websites

A recording, by definition, can be used in different times and places. Few generalisations can be made about the target audience. No wonder songs are mostly recorded in the SL. The insert that often comes with a CD should at least print the ST – even native speakers appreciate the chance to read it, because the singers' lips and gestures cannot be watched, as is possible with video recordings.

Besides, unlike an audience at a concert, people listening to a CD may pause between songs, repeat tracks, alter the volume or balance, read and re-read. One typical context is home listening, with the CD notes available. This difference in situation should permit a song-translator to reduce simplification and to do better justice to the literary features of the text.

Best practice with CDs is to print the ST and TT in parallel or facing-page format, to permit comparisons. An extreme example is a CD in which Jane Thorgren performs songs in eight languages. The notes in the insert give translations for all but the English songs. They are laid out as free verse, unrhymed. Some CD inserts print translations into two languages – or even four.

For translators, the fact that the ST will be printed makes some difference. You may judge that "parallel text" format reduces your freedom to rearrange the line-structure of the original. In practice, translations in recording inserts often choose to observe the line-order of the ST. This makes the pages available for use by the "semi-bilingual" reader: someone with enough sense of the foreign grammar and vocabulary to be truly enlightened by the versions offered. Such readers use translations to understand the SL words, not just the text as a whole.

The translating strategy which best matches this purpose is a sophisticated one acknowledging that the original text is a piece of creative writing. It is not intended for study, however, and is not as free to expand and explicate as a gloss translation may. This is what Newmark calls "semantic translation", in deliberate contrast to "communicative translation". As he conceives it, semantic translation is generally written at the linguistic level of the original author (not the target audience), though it is not inflexible and "may make small concessions to the readership". It takes some account of the aesthetics of the source; it allows for "the translator's intuitive empathy with the original" (1988: 46). Where the text is a fine one, a semantic translation needs to be better than hackwork.

A recent alternative to CD inserts (which cost money and use tiny print) is to place parallel translations on the website of the record company or of the featured singer. This option is increasingly acceptable, since many people are able to read these on a tablet screen or a smartphone. Besides, recorded songs can be purchased by various electronic means, for listening on various portable devices. The situation of such translations seems closer to the CD insert than to the printed concert programme, and so "semantic translations" are the most appropriate. It might be good practice for performing artists, when announcing forthcoming concerts in foreign countries, to place translations of songs online beforehand.

The situation is different, however, in the case of music videos. We can consider these either as songs presented with visual components to be viewed as the song is being sung – or as visually creative videos presented with songs on the soundtrack.

3 Surtitles and subtitles: screen translations to display while the song is being performed

The particular screens in question here are surtitle screens used in live performances. Coined in Canada, the term means "over-title". The screens are usually placed above the stage and display in the language of the audience the words being sung in another language. The electronic display is in white or pale letters on a dark background. Surtitles are commonly used now in opera and music theatre, and sometimes in song recitals. They ought be used more for choir performances. For example when Verdi presented his *Requiem* in 1873, he expected his Italian audience to know enough of what the Latin text meant; but nobody can assume that in the twenty-first century.

Given the need for large lettering (fonts legible from the back of the hall), a typical screen will hold only 32–36 characters per line and a maximum of two lines per caption. This imposes a spatial constraint on the translator, since a long sentence cannot be shown in a single caption, and usually cannot be cut in half. With a divided sentence, one cannot screen the second half without losing the first.

Most audience members use the surtitles provided, either reading every word, or more likely glancing up regularly (like drivers checking the rear-vision mirror) to keep track of the verbal content. It follows that audiences notice when surtitling is badly done: they are likely to complain about cases of bad spacing, incorrect spelling, poor hyphenation, ill-chosen breaks between lines and poor timing (though timing depends mostly on the prompter who operates the computer in real time). They are usually right to complain: surtitles should not be obtrusive for any of these reasons. The translators are actually quite vulnerable: the TT is presented simultaneously with the ST, and so people who know both languages are likely to notice any errors and find them annoying.

Surtitling is like subtitling

The subtitling of films and videos, which has been well known for decades, places written translations low down on the screen of a DVD or TV broadcast. Some of the advice below comes from one of the standard works on this: the Ivarsson and Carroll book *Subtitling* (1998). Surtitling and subtitling are very different from the *skopoi* discussed above, since they involve greater constraints of space and sometimes of time. Translators need to find and use strategies that match these specific problems. With songs, fortunately, the temporal constraints prove manageable. And although the spatial constraints are irksome – they resemble those that translators encounter with cartoons, graphic novels or cramped websites – they seldom prevent good translating. They are much less awkward than the multiple constraints involved in singable translations (see chapters 5 and 6).

Managing time

The time constraints derive chiefly from the speed of the words and the needs of the readers. In practice, they are something like this:

- No caption should be on screen for less than 2 seconds.
- If possible a 1-line caption should be left on screen for at least 3 seconds, a 1.5 for 4 and a full 2-line caption for at least 6.
- There should be a gap of 0.2 seconds between captions.

Since singing delivers words slower than speaking, song titles may stay on screen for 10–15 seconds if the time is available.

Songs are easier to subtitle than feature films in one respect: the words usually arrive quite slowly. So surtitling seldom challenges the audience's reading speed – with some exceptions (e.g. rap) there is time to convey most of the verbal content at comfortable reading speed. There may be places where you give one caption for a repetitive chorus, show it for 15 seconds and then leave the screen blank until new words are needed.

Synchronisation need not be perfect. Begin the caption 0.2 seconds after the line of song, and hold it on after the line is finished if you wish.

One way of sorting out the time factors is with a recording and a stop-watch: by a process called "cueing" (or "spotting" or simply "timing") you mark out the seconds and fractions available for each caption. Usually the musical phrasing and verbal syntax indicate where each caption should start and end. Caption-changes are then marked on a transcript of the song-lyric, which is later used in the performance by the prompter who operates the computer system.

For some people an easier way is to consult the music score and mark these cues in pencil. On each page of a printed piano-vocal score you may identify three places for changing captions, if the tempo is rapid – and maybe nine if the tempo is slow. The words *presto, vivace* and *allegro* mean fast; *adagio, largo* and *lento* mean slow. Surtitles are operated in real time, because live performers vary the tempo, adapting to the hall's acoustic or simply the mood of the moment.

Managing space

The spatial constraints are more demanding. It is not just that the technology offers a maximum of (say) 35 characters per line: it is essential for each caption to be a self-contained statement, ideally a whole sentence. Translations not designed for the screen will very seldom do this well. An apparently short sentence like: "He promised to take me to the dance" fills a whole line of 35 characters.

It is sometimes permissible for translators to divide a long sentence in two. With surtitling it is often highly desirable. Suppose, for example, there is a long complex sentence beginning "although" (a conjunction marking opposition) – you will do well to cut it in two, and start the second sentence with "But". This is quite justifiable, since the *skopos* of surtitles requires simplification of complex

This page (Figure 3.1) comes from the piano score of *Lakmé* by Delibes, words by Gondinet and Gille. The gray circles (really green stickers) indicate exactly when the operator must push the button for the next caption. One is marked B because it is a blank, filling in a 3-second gap. Note that the quick tempo – *allegro agitato* – calls for some 2-line captions, which are needed much less in slow music.

Figure 3.1 Lakmé, music score used in surtitling

syntax and the sacrifice of some complexity. And if the sentence needs to overlap into another caption, you can at least make it reader-friendly. Conjunctions at the start are not advisable. A sentence of over 60 characters like:

"Unless he arrives before the ceremony starts we are in deep trouble"

can become two captions:

1   We need him to arrive before the ceremony starts . . .
2   . . . because otherwise we are in deep trouble

Note the suspension points . . . and the lack of a full stop at the end of the sentence. Note that the first of the two captions makes sense by itself.

Note also that the line-breaks within each caption are well chosen. Two-line captions are needed if the song is wordy and rapid. For the sake of good legibility, you should avoid clumsy breaks: never end the upper line with a determiner or a preposition ("the", "to", "of" etc.). Try not to separate nouns from their adjectives.

Much of the general advice given to subtitlers applies to surtitling also:

- be economical;
- avoid ambiguity;
- make each caption a self-contained statement;
- where this is impossible, break it up judiciously with suspension points;
- use basic punctuation, but ignore full stops at the end of captions;
- be sparing with commas and other punctuation;
- omit obvious repetitions of brief phrases or even whole choruses.

The need for economy, most important in subtitling rapid speech, applies with vocal music also, because of screen size, and the need to be unobtrusive. One usually does a certain amount of condensing and compressing. It is better to under-translate than to try to squeeze every word in. Unimportant words may be ignored; long words should be avoided; short snappy verbs should be favoured – English has many of these. One "boils down" long sentences to retain their key elements. At times one may even choose economy at the expense of naturalness, for example by amending the word "promise" into "vow" (which takes up half the space on screen). Even in languages where the more concise writing-system poses fewer problems of space, one should still try not to overload the audience with verbal content. Some Chinese subtitles set a maximum of 12 characters. A little omission of content is often acceptable in surtitles and subtitles, sometimes essential. The trick there is to omit or change details of little importance, sometimes adjectives, without changing significant ones.

The avoidance of ambiguity, which is good practice in translating generally, matters more than usual in surtitles, because readers have such limited reading time. Beware of homographs, which are common in some languages (e.g. "row" and "row", which look the same). Avoid phrases where the grammar encourages misreading (e.g. "fruit flies like a banana"). And favour formal language over informal, because formal language is usually easier to read quickly – the ST is oral and may involve colloquialisms, but surtitles are a written medium.

Music theatre

With musicals or operas the performance has dramatic and visual dimensions. This makes surtitling more tricky than with an oratorio, or a song recital lacking costume or narrative. The translator devising surtitles for music theatre should have four priorities:

1 first and foremost, to help the audience follow the plot;
2 to enhance audience understanding of the predicaments and emotions of the characters;
3 to blend with the music and the particular production; and
4 to remain unobtrusive.

Given the visual material that the audience is looking at – the set, costumes, gestures etc. – the need to be unobtrusive is great. Nobody goes to a musical in order to read words! People need time to take in the visual components, which may include spectacular effects on a wide stage. That is all the more reason for the surtitles to reduce repetitions and to favour one-liners. In addition, they may omit brief unambiguous utterances whenever there are visible gestures to carry the message. A phrase like "Be off!" may not need a surtitle, since there will surely be a matching gesture translating it non-verbally.

Here is some further good advice, from Judi Palmer:

> Titles must be clear, concise and easy to read, while being incapable of being misconstrued or misunderstood, and they must also be grammatically correct. Idiomatic expressions should only be used sparingly; while these give a sense of character and period, it must be taken into consideration that the titles may be read by someone for whom English is not a first language.
>
> (Palmer 2012: 28)

That last point is well made: a significant minority of people attending musical shows (more than with straight drama) will not be native speakers of their city's main language. Translators working into major world languages like English, Spanish or Mandarin Chinese do well to think about the skill level of their audiences.

Sometimes musicals and operas have words sung off-stage. In that case place these in italics. Sometimes they include duets, in which case you may need a two-line caption with preceded by a dash:

— Has he arrived already?
— Yes, this morning

Here it may be acceptable to add vocatives to clarify who is speaking which words: e.g. "No, Mary, your father is wrong." A strange phenomenon in operas is the presence of trios and quartets where several singers are singing different words. Here one may give few or no captions, since comprehensibility of words is clearly not crucial. More generally, "as opera is a multi-semiotic medium, the intrinsic inadequacies of surtitle text are compensated for by other production elements" (Palmer 2012: 24).

Note that the surtitles for a musical production have to be devised before the first performance, and edited several times. A translator may need to attend some rehearsals in order to be familiar with the concept of the production in question, and to avoid incongruities (such as the phrase "this man" when the singer is pointing to someone on the far side of the stage). As one practitioner puts it: "In the normal run of staged performances, the translation cannot be neutral, but should be in character with, and not contradictory to, the production" (Chambers 2012: 57).

Subtitles on film or video

The captions we call subtitles are similar but not identical to surtitles. They do not have their own screens: they are inserted onto the screen of a film or video, along the bottom. And the subtitling work is done after the visual recording is completed. These facts make for slight differences between surtitles and subtitles. Both kinds of translation need to be economical, so as not to draw attention away from the visual material.

Subtitles should ideally be one-liners. You should try not to occupy too much of the total screen, particularly if it is a TV screen. When two lines are really needed you should try to make the upper one short, so that it intrudes less on the image. A particular problem arises when the lower part of the screen is similar in colour and brightness to the captions, and they "bleed" into the background. Subtitles for TV are generally harder to read than on large cinema screens and should therefore be briefer.

Here are some more quotations from Ivarsson and Carroll:

> Avoid making subtitle breaks between sense blocks, between words that belong together, either logically or grammatically . . . the aim should be to make the breaks coincide with the beginnings and ends of phrases, so that each subtitle forms a coherent unit.
> Straightforward semantic units must be used.
> Obvious repetition of names and common comprehensible phrases need not always be subtitled.
>
> (1998: 90, 157, 158)

One source of difference is dialogue songs: with a live performance a surtitler can find it hard to clarify which words are sung by whom, while a film often shows a close-up of one "singing head" at a time – in which case the surtitler obviously provides that person's words. In most respects, of course, good advice for subtitling applies to surtitling and vice versa. When a live show is filmed and then released on video the subtitles used are likely to be the captions that already served as surtitles, with a few tweaks due to the different technologies. Similarly, if a song performance is accompanied by surtitles and also videoed, then those captions are likely to be suitable for inclusion on YouTube.

Fansubbing

The term "fansubbing" refers to subtitling done by fans, often working in teams. It originated in the vogue for Japanese *anime*, for which fans devised their own non-professional subtitles ("fansubs") for extended works on video. The term now has a wider coverage: many kinds of entertainment media containing words can be fan-subbed, including of course songs and music theatre. Popular music videos, notably from the US, can be fansubbed in the SL (which helps us to follow the words, even if we know English) as well as in popular TLs like Chinese and Japanese.

The guidelines given above for surtitling and subtitling are very relevant to fansubbing. But since the activity is non-professional and rather anarchic, the results are likely to be uneven and sometimes quirky. Some people play around with the colours of their captions – and why not? Some fansubs function as fine tributes to admired songs and artists; and some are parodies, as when a fine song from *My Fair Lady* acquired the subversive caption: "I've thrown a custard in her face."

One of the merits of fansubbing videos is to make the verbal impinge on the visual. The presentation of song videos – itself an interesting, developing art – has tended to draw attention away from the words. Sometimes such clips place the viewer in the excellent position of a audience-member at a live performance; but more often they present multiple images with rapid cutting, so that the visual element trumps and swamps the verbal and sometimes the musical too. Fansubbing restores some prominence to the words.

You may find it fun to do. But don't try to make money out of it – fansubbers are likely to infringe the Berne Convention on copyright material, since the intellectual property (the song and video) will still belong to the original creators.

4 Spoken translations for performers or announcers

There are some singers who like to introduce a foreign song, before performing it in the SL, by reciting a translation. The mezzo-soprano Stephanie Blyth, for example, prefers this to printing a translation in the programmes for her concerts. She thinks (though some beg to differ) that audiences engage more with the song if they're not staring down on bits of paper. This option of recitation is best suited to a high-quality poem or song-lyric. A less ambitious practice is for a presenter to read out a translation, which may be a full version of a short text, or a summary of a longer one. And sometimes radio announcers broadcasting songs use brief introductions giving a little of the song's verbal content.

A translation for this purpose needs to be recitable, of course, and ideally should be devised with this purpose in mind. The text chosen may be a TT made for another *skopos*, like the "programme translations" discussed above. This may work well, particularly if the lyric is short and easy to grasp. But you can probably do better. For one thing, such an intro is oral. Therefore you should:

*   Limit the total length, and make it digestible.
*   Avoid ambiguities, e.g. homophones ("sun" sounds like "son").
*   Avoid obscurities and complex syntax.
*   Exploit the possible emphases of spoken delivery: underlining is usually avoided with printed words, but is good for texts that will be spoken.

Imagine, for example, that some Australian folk musicians are performing in San Diego and wish to finish their concert with a partly acted version of "Waltzing Matilda", which is their national song. This ballad is not short. To present its verbal content, they might prepare the following intro – to be spoken first in Spanish and then in standard English (since the song contains historic slang):

> *The title means something like "Walking the countryside carrying a bag". It's also the chorus: please join in! The story tells of a swagman (that's a hobo) who camps by a billabong (that's a pond). Along comes a jumbug (that's a sheep) and he grabs it for its meat. Then along comes the sheriff to catch him for sheep-stealing. So to avoid arrest he dives into the pond. The song ends with his ghost singing "Waltzing Matilda".*

That example, though rather long for a spoken intro, would surely enhance the enjoyment of the song, and could even be made entertaining in itself. Australians enjoy singing this ballad much more than their official national anthem. But audiences who are not given some initiation into the song's narrative content may find it puzzling and tiresome.

The example uses what some call "gist translation". It's a mixture of translation and précis. It renders the main sense and feeling of the words without too much detail, focusing in this case on the storyline. It deliberately summarises. It tries to communicate quickly and directly, since re-reading is not possible. Gist translation is the opposite of "gloss translation" (above). And it uses a style that would be less appropriate for a written text on paper or on screen.

That example of "Waltzing Matilda" clarifies a few terms for the audience's benefit, a legitimate component of good translating. In addition, this kind of oral text can give incidental information beyond what is strictly translating. For some songs it may be useful to say:

*   This piece was written as a protest against . . .
*   She wrote this as a tribute to a close friend who died suddenly.
*   This song arose from the Canterbury earthquakes of 2010–11.

Such details resemble the footnotes recommended in a study translation, but presented in an oral intro. This can improve rapport with audiences, for example at folk concerts or outdoor festivals, where printed programmes are not used.

Scholars have given little attention to this kind of translation, perhaps because it is relatively informal and sometimes just improvised, with or without a quiet instrumental backing. But it needed to be included in the present chapter, which has focused on the range of situations in which TTs might be used. In many cases it would be a good idea for musicians themselves to devise such spoken texts. Even singers with limited knowledge of the SL should be encouraged to wrestle with the words, as part of their overall preparation for presenting a song. There are real artistic benefits to be gained from imposing this task on the performer (who may of course consult a native speaker or a printed translation). But it would be easier for a translator to devise such a version.

Exercise (A) – Study translation

Prepare a "study translation" for a soprano whose English is not strong. She wants to perform a bracket of lullabies in different languages, and needs to include something lively (this text, by Thomas Randolph c1630, has music by Benjamin Britten 1947). The song can be heard at http://www.youtube.com/watch?v=ZW8JvmchuBU

A charm

Quiet! Sleep! or I will make
Erinnys whip thee with a snake,
And cruel Rhadamanthus take
Thy body to the boiling lake,
Where fire and brimstones never slake;
Thy heart shall burn, thy head shall ache,
And ev'ry joint about thee quake;
And therefore dare not yet to wake!
Quiet, sleep! Quiet, sleep! Quiet!

Quiet! Sleep! or thou shalt see
The horrid hags of Tartary,
Whose tresses ugly serpents be,
And Cerberus shall bark at thee,
And all the Furies that are three
The worst is called Tisiphone,
Shall lash thee to eternity;
And therefore sleep thou peacefully
Quiet, sleep! Quiet, sleep! Quiet!

Exercise (B) – Study or programme translation

Consider this nineteenth-century English sonnet, "Silent Noon", which has been set to music several times, notably by Vaughan Williams. Listen to it at http://www.youtube.com/watch?v=2FGeLUQQH6w

Silent Noon

Your hands lie open in the long fresh grass, –
The finger-points look through like rosy blooms:
Your eyes smile peace. The pasture gleams and glooms
'Neath billowing clouds that scatter and amass.
All round our nest, far as the eye can pass,
Are golden kingcup fields with silver edge
Where the cow-parsley skirts the hawthorn hedge.
'Tis visible silence, still as the hour-glass.

Deep in the sun-searched growths the dragon-fly
Hangs like a blue thread loosened from the sky: –
So this winged hour is dropt to us from above.
Oh! clasp we to our hearts, for deathless dower,
This close-companioned inarticulate hour
When twofold silence was the song of love.

– D. G. Rossetti

(a) If you are a native speaker of English, make a "study translation" of it, for the sake of a singer whose English is limited but who is keen to really "get inside" the text. Try to follow the guidelines above. Think of yourself not as a poem-translator, but as a language consultant.
(b) If English is not your native language, imagine that a British singer will be performing it in some foreign city and has commissioned you to make a translation for the programme notes. Try to make it reader-friendly, yet still somewhat poetic.

Alternatively, instead of a programme translation, imagine you have been asked to make a translation for a CD insert (c), or surtitles for the performance (d) or subtitles for a videoed version (e).

Exercise (C) – Spoken translation

It has been asserted that: "No singer should sing a foreign song in the SL without being able to introduce it in the language of the audience with a few words explaining its verbal content." Do you accept this assertion as a general rule? Would you make any objections or exceptions?

Further reading

1 *On* Skopos *Theory*

A good general book in English on functionalist thinking is:

Nord, Christiane (1997) *Translating as a Purposeful Activity*, Manchester, St Jerome.
  More ambitious are:
Reiss, Katharina & Vermeer, H. J. (1984) *Grundlegung einer allgemeinen Translationstheorie*, Tübingen, Niemeyer.
Reiss, Katharina & Vermeer, H. J. (2014) *Towards a General Theory of Translational Action: Skopos Theory Explained*, London, Routledge.
Vermeer, H. J. (1989) "Skopos and Commission in Translational Action", in Venuti, L. (ed) (2000) *The Translation Studies Reader*. London & New York, Routledge, 221–232.
The chart of functional strategies originates in Low, Peter (2003) "Translating Poetic Songs: An Attempt at a Functional Account of Strategies" in *Target* 15/1: 95–115.
A shorter exposé aimed at singers is Low, Peter (2006) "Translations of Songs – Which Kind Matches Your Purpose?" in *Journal of Singing* 62/5: 505–513. The article "Purposeful Translating" in Helen Minors (2012) covers similar ground in the context of a major case study: the texts used by Benjamin Britten in his very varied vocal music.

2 *Compendiums of translations of classical songs*

Bernac, Pierre (1970) *The Interpretation of French Song*, London, Gollancz.
Fischer-Dieskau, D. (1977) *The Fischer-Dieskau Book of Lieder*, New York, Knopf.
Johnson, Graham & Stokes, Richard (1999) *A French Song Companion*, Oxford, OUP. See also www.lieder.net/
Miller, Philip (ed) (1963) *The Ring of Words, an Anthology of Song Texts*, New York, Norton.

3 *Surtitling*

Low, Peter (2002) "Surtitles for Opera, A Specialised Translating Task" in *Babel* 48/2: 97–110.
Music, Text and Translation ed. Helen Minors (2012), articles by J. Palmer "Surtitling Opera: A Surtitler's Perspective on Making and Breaking the Rules"; by J. Page "Surtitling Opera: A Translator's Perspective"; and by K. Chambers: "Assistance or Obstruction: Translated Text in Opera Performances."
Sario, M. & Oksanen, S. (1996) "Le sur-titrage des opéras à l'opéra national de Finlande" in Gambier, Y. (ed) *Les Transferts linguistiques dans les médias audio-visuels*, Paris, Presses Universitaires.

4 *Subtitling*

Díaz Cintas, Jorge & Remael, Aline (2007 & 2014) *Audiovisual Translation: Subtitling*, Manchester, St. Jerome.
Ivarsson, Jan & Carroll, Mary (1998) *Subtitling*, Simrishamn, Transedit.

References

Chambers, Kenneth (2012) "Assistance or Obstruction: Translated Text in Opera Performances" in Minors (2012).

Ezust, Emily (2012) http://www.sparksandwirycries.com/FeaturedArticles/EmilyEzust-ThoughtsonthegentleartoftranslatingArtSongtexts.aspx

Ezust, Emily (2015) The LiederNet Archive http://www.lieder.net/lieder/index.html

Ivarsson, Jan & Carroll, Mary (1998) *Subtitling*, Simrishamn, Transedit.

Palmer, Judi (2012) "Surtitling Opera: A Surtitler's Perspective on Making and Breaking the Rules" in Minors (2012).

Low, Peter (2012) "Purposeful Translating – The Case of Britten's Vocal Music" in Minors (2012), 101–115.

Minors, Helen (ed) (2012) *Music, Text and Translation*, London, Bloomsbury.

Newmark, Peter (1988) *A Textbook of Translation*, New York, Prentice Hall.

Nida, Eugene (1964) *Toward a Science of Translating*, Leiden, Brill.

Nord, Christiane (1997) *Translating as a Purposeful Activity*, Manchester, St Jerome.

Paton, John Glenn (2006) *Foundations of Singing: A Guidebook to Vocal Technique and Song Interpretation*, Boston, MA, McGraw-Hill.

Paton, John Glenn (2003, November) Personal communication.

Phillips, Lois (1979) *Lieder Line by Line, and Word for Word*, London, Duckworth.

Vermeer, H. J. (1989) "Skopos and Commission in Translational Action" in Venuti, L. (ed) (2000), *The Translation Studies Reader*, London & New York, Routledge.

4 "Downstream" difficulties

The "downstream" problems of devising the target text

Chapter 2 gave most attention to the problems located within source texts, usually problems of meaning. But problems are located also in the translation process: a word or sentence which was straightforward in the SL may resist translation into some or all TLs.

One metaphor for this process is a sea-voyage: a ST located in one country (one language) needs to travel to another, across an ocean which may be rough, and may seem to be affected by different gravitational fields. As a result, the cargo with which it set off – the content and intent of the ST – is found to be mysteriously transformed on arrival in the foreign port. Many things are lost in transit, and here is an incomplete list of them:

- the particular vowels of the SL
- the consonants of the ST
- the particular word-order
- the precise grammar (e.g. parts of speech)
- the exact length in characters or syllable-count
- the complete and accurate meaning.

Fortunately the translator is not tasked with ensuring the survival of every single item of cargo, which would be impossible, but with preserving *all the most valuable items*, even at the expense of others. When you translate ordinary informative texts this is usually easy to discern: the meaning is the valuable bit. It can be much harder with song-lyrics – oral texts where the sounds of the words certainly matter, and where the tone of the words (affectionate, sarcastic or whatever) is often important. Besides, people may hold conflicting views about which items of cargo are essential and which are not. That is all the more reason to examine the ST carefully to judge what matters most – as recommended in chapter 2 – and also to consider how the intended purpose of the TT can dictate or affect your strategy and tactics, as recommended particularly in chapter 3.

Let us extend this sea-transit metaphor: there is cargo that seems mysteriously to come on board during the voyage: unwanted things which may be metaphorically termed "stowaways". These may involve meaning or sound. They often introduce ambiguity. For example a precise pronoun in the ST may become an "it" with two possible antecedents, or an unambiguous ST sentence may emerge in English as: "she only watches TV at home", where it's unclear whether the "only" refers to the activity or the place or the thing watched. The main remedy for such "stowaways" is to build in a good editing process. This should include a late stage where you put the ST to the side and look at your TT *just as a text in the TL* – which after all is what your readers will be doing. It is best to delay this stage until some time after your main translating work, so that you are less influenced by your knowledge of the ST. You may then discover that some of your phrases are unexpectedly clumsy, obscure or ambiguous.

The worst "stowaways" may even act as "hijackers", taking control of the meaning in the TL. For example the innocent English phrase "our neighbours who go fishing" might in French become *nos voisins qui pêchent* – which sounds the same as *nos voisins qui pèchent* (our neighbours who sin)! There are various possible reasons for stowaways and hijackers, such as homophones in the TL – as in this example – or unwanted associations. The problem, of course, is that they intrude, distract and derail.

Another area of difficulty in re-coding is that some verbal features which are natural and elegant in the SL just cannot be made natural and elegant in the TL. To understand the French word *dont* (or the German word *doch*) is relatively easy: to translate it elegantly is difficult. And clumsiness needs to be avoided, because it makes the language sound phony. This might not matter in a birth certificate, but a song-text has much more emotional investment. When singers are to perform in a SL they don't know well, they need to understand why the text was deemed suitable for singing, and will not be helped by a clumsy TT (or Google Translate) – so you must try to tell them. And when singers are to perform singable translations they need language that sings and dances.

The specifics of the target language

All translators need to know their TL well, and song-translators need to be real wordsmiths, adept at manipulating the language they work with, resourceful at finding several ways of saying something in that language and discerning in selecting best option. The ability to generate two or more solutions to a verbal problem is crucial, and so is the ability to choose well between them.

Let us briefly consider one case – English. This is quite a good language to translate into: its huge vocabulary certainly helps. For any foreign phrase it is usually possible to find several translation options, with or without recourse to a thesaurus (a word-book or online resource not found in all languages, which goes beyond synonyms into wider lexical fields). For a simple word like "foolish", indeed, an English thesaurus can list thirty near-synonyms to choose from. There are problems of register, admittedly: some areas of the large lexicon are too formal and Latinate to be very useful in songs. Yet even this has an advantage: the translator can, for example, deliberately choose the Latinate verb "tolerate" rather than its less formal synonym "put up with".

English can be very concise. The ability to say something in very few syllables is a great asset for song-translators. The availability of many short expressive verbs (such as "scrub" or "drub") is a boon when you're translating into English – and a difficulty when moving out of English (as mentioned in chapter 2).

All languages present grammatical problems. English, being relatively unin-flected, relies more on word-order than do some other languages. Its strong SVO pattern (subject-verb-object) can be restrictive, for example if you want to put the verb first. Besides, certain possibilities that do exist in English should be used very sparingly with songs – passives, for example, or the pronoun "one" when used as a dummy subject in phrases like "One often finds . . .". English has an annoying habit of turning an elegant line in a foreign song into something crude and clumsy, for example the French phrase *Ils s'écrivent* emerges with seven syl-lables: "They write to one another." Yet there are welcome areas of flexibility, such as the freedom to exploit existing prefixes and suffixes for new terms: a song-translator may even create novel but transparent phrases like "We will out-laugh you" or "She is so friendable". This is possible, albeit a bit odd; most other languages are more resistant to such manipulation.

That's enough about the case of English. The general point is that every TL has its own idiosyncrasies, and every TL can handle some things better than others. In every TL a translator should strive, despite the constraints of the ST, to write naturally.

The challenge of naturalness

The term "naturalness" is not uncommon in discussions of translation, but deserves to be used more. The basic assumption here is that a TT needs to be natural in the sense of being *a text that could have been created spontaneously in the TL* – by a songwriter, poet or other wordsmith within the target culture. Even specialist legal or scientific texts should be turned into TTs that are relatively natural, at least to their specialist readers, TTs that don't go against the grain of the language. Note that this does not mean "plain colloquial diction", since good writers in any lan-guage are never limited to that. But what it clearly excludes is stilted language – the sort of clumsy writing that is sometimes called "translationese" because it is produced by bad translators (whether humans or machines) and never by people who actually think and write in the TL. One of the sources of translationese is the aberrant schoolroom notion that "literal translations" (seldom defined) are best and most accurate.

Naturalness is part of a broader translating principle: *observe the norms of the TL*. The notable theorists Nida and Taber said that translators should seek the "closest natural equivalent" in the TL (1969: 12). This should apply generally to song-translating – though not universally, as we shall see.

It was not always observed in the past. The clumsiness of poor rhymesters used to result in obscurity, fractured pronunciation, inappropriate slang or archaisms and ridiculous word-order. Their strategic errors were to ignore naturalness and to prioritise rhyme. An extended attack on this was made as long ago as 1852 by Richard Wagner, who wrote scornfully about translations used in German opera-houses. Now Wagner, a major opera composer, was also a notable librettist: he wrote all the words to his *Ring der Nibelungen*. Here is the passage from his *Oper und Drama*:

> These translations [. . .] put together by people who knew nothing of either music or poetry [. . .] were before all else not musical; they rendered an Italian or French text-book, for itself as word-poem, into a so-called Iambic metre which they ignorantly took to represent the really quite unrhythmic measure of the original; and these verses they got written under the music by some poor hack of a music-copyist, with instructions to dribble out a syllable to every note.
>
> The poetical labours of the translator had consisted in furnishing the vulgarest prose with the absurdest end-rhymes; and since he had often had the most painful difficulty in finding these rhymes themselves, – all heedless that they would be almost inaudible in the music, – his love toward them had made him distort the natural order of the words, past any hope of understanding. This hateful Verse, contemptible and muddled in itself, was now laid under a music whose distinctive Accents it nowhere fitted; on lengthy notes there came short syllables, on longer syllables the shorter notes; on the musical 'ridge' there came the verse's 'hollow', and so the other way round. From these grossest offences against the sound, the translation passed on to a complete distortion of the latter on the ear, by countless textual repetition, that the ear instinctively turned away from the text and devoted its sole attention to the purely melodic utterance.
>
> (1893: 359–360)

One thing highlighted here is the question of rhyme (a matter to be considered later, in chapter 6). Another is word-order, where Wagner criticises the translations for their lack of naturalness and the loss of comprehensibility. A more subtle issue is the problem of mismatch between verbal and musical phrases (his point about ridge and hollow). A much more recent discussion of bad German TTs speaks of "bombastic clichés and hackneyed phraseology, inverted syntax, displaced accents, distorted rhythm and other infelicitous *ad hoc* solutions" (Gorlée 1997: 247). How could the singers begin to perform such lyrics with the sincerity and conviction that good drama requires?

No better than the nineteenth-century German translations which Wagner loathed are the English ones done in the same period. Theodore Baker's version of *Die schöne Müllerin* (words by Müller, music by Schubert) appeared in 1895 and remained in print for much of the twentieth century. Here is part of song six "Der Neugierige":

O Bächlein, meiner Liebe	*O streamlet dearest streamlet,*
Wie bist du heut so stumm!	*How dumb thou art today,*
Will ja nur Eines wissen,	*I'd fain know one thing only,*
Ein Wörtchen um und um,	*One word then prythee say.*

Translations such as this betray a failure to assess the naturalness of both ST and TT. In translations made by Baker and his contemporaries one often finds adjectives placed after nouns and archaisms where none were present in the ST. Some of these versions were made by translators who knew both languages well, yet poor strategy made the results unusable – and may even have led some people to the view that all song-translations are inevitably bizarre or ridiculous. It is still possible now to encounter a translation which, as one singer puts is: "doesn't sound like anything I've ever heard a human being say in English" (Flood 2015). This might not matter in a medical article, but song is more demanding: "the singer needs words that may be sung with sincerity" (Graham 1989: 35).

The criterion requiring a translator to use the TL in a reasonably natural way is linked particularly with the translator's duty to the audience – the future receivers of the musico-verbal message. This duty requires, almost always, that the TT should not read like a translation. Now there is a wide debate, in literary translation, about whether a TT should conceal the fact that it has been translated, or instead remain close to the ST in register and language (a contrast sometimes called "covert" or "overt"). Some recommend the latter option for literary texts; few would claim that a difficult idiosyncratic poem can be adequately rendered by a version full of "reader-friendly" blandness. But song is a different case from poetry, because a printed poem can be read slowly and re-read, whereas a song-text needs to communicate fast and effectively (except in a study translation). This places a greater premium on naturalness of language, because unnaturalness demands from the audience additional and superfluous processing effort. A singable TT is not worth making unless it can be understood while the song is sung.

This is not to claim that song-translations must avoid unnatural English at all costs: merely that naturalness is one of the criteria which the translator must strive for. As Ernst-August Gutt says in more general terms:

> "Unnaturalness" in translated texts often seems to involve gratuitous processing effort on the receptor audience's part: perhaps due to interference from the original language or insufficient mastery of the receptor language, the expression used by the translator may turn out to require more than optimal processing cost on the audience's part.
>
> (1991: 389)

In songs, of course, processing time cannot be lengthened at will.

It follows that you should try not to use rare words, since they reduce the naturalness of a text. Usually one translates common SL words into common TL words. And song-lyrics, more than most texts, depend for their emotional effects on common words – e.g. verbs and nouns for basic feelings and common experiences. In English these are short words of Anglo-Saxon origin.

In some cases the need for naturalness should put you on guard against cognate terms (look-alike words with the same origin). If the Italian word *calumnia* is translated as "calumny", we cannot fault it on grounds of etymology or meaning, yet we must reject it because of its rarity and formality. The ordinary English word is "slander", and other options are available, such as "smear". Similarly, if the Spanish word *mejorar* is translated with the cognate "ameliorate", that is a bad choice, because what people actually say in English is "improve". Those are extreme examples, yet there must be hundreds of such cases in languages with large lexicons.

Those two examples are not "false friends" (cognates diverging in meaning). But they should be rejected as "clumsy cognates". These are a particular problem in English, which be called an "upstairs/downstairs language". Over the centuries, English imported many high-flown Latinate words on top of the more earthy Germanic equivalents. Typically, the Latinate word is used less often, has more syllables and has a higher social register than its Anglo-Saxon synonym (it is more learned, more formal). A good example is "liberty": though not a rare word, it's certainly used much less than the Anglo-Saxon "freedom" (less than 23% as much, according to the British National Corpus [BNC], an excellent tool for finding word-frequencies in English: http://www.natcorp.ox.ac.uk/). Therefore *libertad* and its cognates in other Romance languages should normally be translated as "freedom". Consider this remark:

> Some translators seem to think that if a Latinate word has the same meaning in French and English that it is necessarily appropriate to make the straight substitution, never mind the fact that the stress is always then placed on the WRONG syLLABle, and that lyrics in English tend to work better with more Anglo-Saxon and less Latin-sounding words.
>
> (Flood 2015)

Conversely, the English verb "congratulate" should not be rendered by its French cognate *congratuler*, because French people hardly ever use it – their natural choice is *féliciter.*

That advice to choose common words, words frequently used in the TL, does not apply, however, when the SL word itself is rare. For a rare word in the ST, for example a scientific term, you will turn to a rare TL word. And how do you know whether a word is rare or common? The short answer is that native speakers "just know". That's one of the reasons why you should normally translate into your first language, or at least have your work checked by a native speaker of the TL, someone better able to assess your naturalness of style, without reference to databases such as the BNC.

Certain elements of naturalness are harder to detect: for example the natural use of plurals as against singulars. The English word "progress" is singular, yet the normal equivalent in some languages is plural. Conversely, to make generalisations, English prefers the plural to the singular. Can we say: "the kea is a mountain parrot"? Yes, but in English the plural is more natural: "keas are . . .". With a sentence like *El catalán entiende castellano* a translator is not bound by the SL grammar: "The Catalan understands Spanish", but should find whatever is natural in the TL. In English the answer is: "Catalans understand Spanish." Although such awkwardness may seem minor, it becomes serious when sub-optimal choices become numerous and weaken the TT as a whole.

For naturalness, the usual evaluative questions are these: "Is this a piece of normal standard English? (or Spanish or whatever)". "Is this well-written in the TL?" Note that this criterion is not limited to translations: we can ask of any text how natural it is. Naturalness, in this sense, is culture-specific and time-bound. Usages and conventions evolve in all living languages. Besides, some languages not only have more flexibility (for example in basic word-order), but are also more tolerant of deviations in this matter.

For assessing naturalness there is no total objectivity. If you want to judge whether your TT scores well on naturalness, your best option would be to seek assessments from several native-speakers of the TL, and then aggregate their responses (like judges of acrobatics). The result will not be objective, but will carry the weight of consensus.

Creative deviations

What if a song-text exhibits creative deviations from standard language? Although most songwriters in English today use the current spoken language, that has not been true of all times and places. The criterion of naturalness certainly does not insist on common conversational language where the ST itself is non-conversational. With deviations the translator is entitled – and probably advised – to play a similar deviant game. Basically, if you encounter a ST featuring deliberately non-standard language, you need to ask why it has that character, and consider whether your translation needs to replicate that feature.

In fact many song-lyrics in many languages use words in unusual, creative, even bizarre ways – and do so deliberately. We wouldn't want a translator to reduce all deviance to a smooth "blandspeak". So if a ST contains a newly coined word – for example "soothest sleep" in a poem by Keats – the translator should consider the possibility of a neologism in the TL. How would you handle the collocation "material girl" coined by Madonna? And how would you cope with "cry me a river" (in a jazz classic), where the transitive use of the verb "cry" is a striking deviation from the norm?

One strange feature of old song-translations into English, before about 1940, was archaism: for example German songs using the pronouns "du" and "dich" were rendered with "thou" and "thee", even though these pronouns were unused except in church. Yet "du" and "dich" were and are everyday pronouns in German – and so the translators were adding archaism onto STs which lacked it. This was bizarre and unnatural, and it reduced the usefulness of the TTs.

Suppose you are asked to translate some sixteenth-century French poems by Marot, set to music 400 years later by Georges Enescu. The texts certainly look archaic to the modern eye, but that is irrelevant. The key point is that they contain no deliberate archaisms: the poet was simply using the French of his own day. What the modern reader perceives as archaism was not intrinsic to the ST. It would be wrong, therefore, to produce an archaic TT saying "thou vouchsafest". No, the text was in contemporary sixteenth-century language, and so a translator should use current language now, though without any new twenty-first-century terms, which would strike people as anachronistic. A good tool to check the recentness of words and phrases before 2008 is https://books.google.com/ngrams – it charts frequencies of thousands of words in eight languages. Conversely, the situation where archaic language is most justified is where the ST itself contained that unnatural feature from the beginning.

The outmoded English verb "to slay", for example, might be rendered in French by the archaic verb *occire* and not the normal *tuer* "to kill". Yet the Broadway musical *The Man of La Mancha* – 1964, after Cervantes – which deliberately used some Shakespearean phrases, was translated into straight modern French by a team (Jacques Brel and others) who clearly judged that its archaic features were not crucial.

To domesticate or not?

What might be called "the domestication debate" concerns the recurrent question of whether translators should retain all the foreignness of a foreign text, and to what extent they should "bring the text to the reader" by replacing foreign details with details of the target culture. This is different from the question of "overt or covert" (whether the TT should conceal its linguistic character as a translation); a significant part of it is the question of whether a TT should alter the cultural references found in the ST. This issue is important with songs, because many of them are deeply embedded in a particular place and culture, and because translators, during the process of re-coding the lyric into another language, may be tempted to supplement linguistic transfer – into a natural style of the TL – with cultural transfer. For example they may wish to translate "shekels" as dollars.

The culture-specific details you may encounter can be very varied: names of places and people, foods and drinks, clothing and housing terms, names of sports and festivals, brand names, religious terms, even coins and measures. A similar term sometimes used is "culture-bound"; but if that implies the item cannot be "untied" from its location, then it makes a hasty and perhaps false assumption. In the past, for example, pizza was specific to Italy and alien elsewhere, but now it has certainly broken loose!

One approach to such details can be called purist: retain all the foreignness. With names this means calling Giovanni Giovanni and Zdenek Zdenek, calling Lisboa and Москва Lisboa and Moskva. These choices show great respect for the source culture. Some theorists call this purist approach "foreignising" (*verfremden* in German), yet the term is ill-chosen. The practice does not in fact *confer* foreignness on anything which wasn't foreign already – it is merely a refusal to domesticate.

The contrary approach is found particularly in children's books: a little story about a peasant family in Kazakhstan may be transformed, domesticated, into a US scene resembling *Little House on the Prairie*, with American names, foods, animals etc. until nothing remains that actually smells of Central Asia. In its extreme form, domestication shows a reluctance to present anything strange or foreign, for fear that people might dislike it or not cope with it – a reluctance that misjudges people generally and children in particular.

A major figure in this debate, Lawrence Venuti, attacks those practices whereby all traces of foreignness or otherness are purposely erased from a text. Finding this undesirable in literary translating, he is very willing for readers of translations to encounter "resistant" elements in the translating style and in the cultural details. One major value of his argument has been its challenge to domesticating translators: Why ever should Giovanni be turned into "John"? Why ever should you pander to your readers' possible dislike of this foreign reference or this unusual turn of phrase?

Venuti argues strongly against what he repeatedly calls the "ethnocentric violence of domestication". Yet he admits that "in the translating process, foreign languages, texts, and cultures will always undergo some degree and form of reduction, exclusion, and inscription" (1995: 310). This is not an all-or-nothing matter.

Should song-translators domesticate? To some extent, yes. The present chapter has tended to advocate "natural" language without any resistant elements, arguing that the genre of song generally requires language that is easily processed. But that was not intended to produce song-translations with no foreign elements: on the contrary, one reason for translating songs is precisely the fact that *good songs are produced by cultures other than yours*. Hence a sort of challenge: try not to domesticate culture-specific items, unless you can state very good reasons.

Try to keep the original names rather than domesticating them. If you turn an Italian love-song about Lucia into an English song about Lucy or Lulu, then its foreignness is lessened, usually for no benefit, and its charm is reduced. The Gershwin song "I Loves You Porgy" cannot become *Te quiero Pablo* without losing a key feature (though in Spanish this unusual name should probably be spelt "Porguy"). Do retain proper names, unless there is a very good reason not to. If people say "That's unpronounceable", don't believe them! This applies to placenames too: nowadays geographical names in Europe tend to be standardised to their local versions – Roma, München etc. – though fantasy place-names may be translated fancifully.

What of other cultural details? If a French song uses the phrase *prendre un pastis avec moi*, the domesticator who puts "have a beer with me" would be reducing the Frenchness of the song. Is not the simple phrase "drink a pastis with me" a better option, even for people who have never tasted pastis? Now imagine a song that refers to a religious festival or cultural event, such as Diwali, the Hajj, el Día de los Reyes or Hanukkah. Before exploring ways of domesticating that reference into the culture you are targeting, ask yourself whether retaining the original SL term is a viable option, and if not why not. You may well identify a problem of comprehensibility; but you should not assume that such problems are insurmountable. The Mexican ceremony evoked in *Cantos para las posadas*, for example, may not be familiar elsewhere (it's a parade re-enacting Joseph and Mary's attempts to find lodging in Bethlehem), but can surely be understood wherever people have heard of Christmas. Domestication incurs a cost and is often unnecessary.

The one situation where domesticating is always wrong is that of the "study translation", where culture-specific items can be explained at some length. The situation where it is most likely to be justified is the most constrained *skopos*:

singable translations. But even here when it proves impossible to retain source-culture elements, the use of target-culture elements is not the only alternative: culture-specific details can often be replaced by universal or neutral ones.

So, although this chapter has generally argued for the choice of natural language to suit the TL audience, it inclines towards the retention of culture-specific elements from the ST, even when they seem foreign. How foreign are they, really? We live in a global village, buffeted by winds from many quarters. Those who translate out of English know that their target audiences are often encountering English words, elements of US culture and many other kinds of foreignness – or soon will be. And we who translate into English ought to know that our audiences also face elements of other cultures in their lives, elements that deserve to be acknowledged and welcomed. All human beings need to evolve towards being global citizens; and translators (who in this matter are generally more advanced than the average) have a role in helping people to learn and accept this.

Which option?

There's a lyric by Prévert in which someone commits suicide by leaping off the Tour St-Jacques, a former church-tower in Paris. How would you prefer to translate it? And how would you justify your preference?

(a) *From the Tour St-Jacques I threw myself. . .* (purist)
(b) *From the Golden Gate Bridge I threw myself. . .* (domesticating)
(c) *From the Eiffel Tower I threw myself* (compromise: still in Paris, but familiar to everyone)
(d) None of the above: yet another option.

For and against the source language

Before proceeding, let us consider another debate: whether songs should be sung in the source language (as was assumed in chapter 3) or whether they may be legitimately and effectively performed in "singable translations". This is something of a digression, inasmuch as decisions about performance are not made by translators but by musicians. Yet the topic is too important and too controversial to omit. Besides, chapters 5 and 6 will be assuming that singable translations have a place, at least sometimes.

In favour of the source language

Those who think songs should be performed in the SL tend to cite the strong claim of that original language: only the ST offers the actual words written by the songwriter and used by the composer (who may well be the same person). No translation will retain the full content and intent of those words, let alone retain all its phonic features – rhymes and vowel-sounds, effects of rhythm, and all the textures of the SL.

This view is particularly strong in some devotees of German Lieder. They at times assert that a song-text by Goethe must never be sung except in the original German. In an extreme form this resembles religious dogma – like a Muslim saying that the Holy Quran must not be recited in any language but Arabic. A more typical expression of it is this, from Kenneth Whitton: "To sing Lieder in translation is a weak substitute for the real thing – a poor supermarket wine beside one of the great Rhine or Rhine-Hessian vintages!" (1984: 85) How could it be the "real thing" without the source text? Such people either understand German or are happy to receive the songs' verbal content on printed programs.

The view is strong also in devotees of Italian opera: they want to hear the open syllables and clear vowels of Italian, and are happy for the verbal meanings to be conveyed as projected surtitles, which they may well choose to ignore. It follows also that young singers hoping to break into opera need to prove their competence in Italian, German and French, and therefore choose to avoid singing translations from these languages (but may agree to sing Russian or Scandinavian songs in English).

There is also a strong pragmatic argument for singing in the SL – the dubious quality of many so-called singable translations, or simply their non-existence. There are many cases, indeed, where this argument must be a clinching one . . . until such time as a usable TT is devised.

A different argument applies to folk music. A traditional song from Africa or Asia – for example a harvest song or a wedding song – may be performed with folk instruments as an item of artistic heritage, a specimen of a particular culture and perhaps of an endangered language. In such cases, obviously, the SL has a strong claim on the grounds of linguistic and ethnic authenticity. Yet such performances lose a different kind of authenticity: the audience is hearing not words charged with meaning but merely sounds that tell them next to nothing.

Against the source language

Other people contend that they wish to learn the meaning of the song's words not from a surtitle or a printed program but out of the singer's mouth. The opera producer David Pountney puts it this way: "the sense arrives, like a glowing hot coal, straight from the mouth of the singer, and strikes instantly at the head and heart of the listener" (1975: ix). Similarly, the Israeli scholar and translator Harai Golomb describes singing in translation, as "the only procedure that can possibly simulate the effect of synchronised verbal/music/rhetorical fusion, as it functions in the original, transmitted from a singer's mouth to a listener's ear as an interaction realised in sound, sense and gesture" (2005: 142).

Part of this argument is the contention that when purists dismiss a singable TT as "a weak substitute for the real thing" (Whitton, quoted above), they are begging the question, making a dubious assumption. Reality is complex, and whenever the meanings of the ST are not being communicated directly to an audience, a

significant piece of reality is lost. The original "real thing", surely, was a performance in which the singer conveyed both words and music simultaneously to the
listeners' *ears and brains*, and where words and music combined to achieve a
simultaneous emotional effect. Songwriters usually want the audience to understand and not just hear!

Translation does of course change the vowels and consonants. Occasionally the
essence of a song may lie in specific phonic or cultural features. But not often:
these are generally incidental. Are the nasal vowels common in French and Portuguese really essential features? Are the consonants which in German are spelt
SCH and CH really key features of all songs in that language? Do the particular
inflexions of Japanese constitute essential elements in their songs? Almost never.
A substitute is not weak if it delivers nearly everything of importance!

Listeners to popular music seem much more willing to accept singable translations. When a long ballad is sung in country-and-western style to an audience
in Memphis, Tennessee, there is a total "real thing", which includes the audience's involvement, and which cannot be replicated for listeners who cannot
follow the song's narrative. Folksingers in (say) Argentina would not hesitate to
perform the ballad in Spanish, since their audiences would be happy to receive
the "authentic story" in a singable translation, at the cost of the "authentic phonemes" of the ST.

The songs that benefit most from performance in the language of the audience
are logocentric ones, in particularly narrative songs, dramatic songs and comic
songs. With poor timing, a surprise is weakened, and a joke can fall completely
flat – both come best straight from the singer's mouth into the hearer's mind. And
only a good singable translation can provide that optimal timing. Good singers
can (metaphorically) underline or italicise words in various ways not available in
print. Besides, singers deliver words best in the language(s) they know really well.

The crucial point, however, is whether or not listeners ignorant of the SL receive
an authentic experience of the song, one in which its musical dimension is linked
to a verbal dimension which, on the whole, does it justice. A minority of singable
translations come close to achieving this; many more could do so in future, if
more skilful translators applied better strategies.

To return to the case of Lieder: it is not surprising that German-speaking listeners, those who have immediate access to Goethe's actual words, find his texts
unsatisfying in another language. This observation – which applies in other languages also – highlights an important general point: *speakers of the SL are not the
target audience for song-translations!* It's obvious, really: the usual purpose of
translating is to make a text in one SL available to people who do not know that
language. Speakers of the SL are therefore the wrong people to evaluate song-
translations (except in respect of accuracy of Sense).

Burton Raffel's book on poetry-translating puts it this way: "*no translation is,
was, or ever will be the original which it translates* [his emphasis]. The interpreta-
tive translator faces this uncrossable gulf and tries to give the reader as much of
the original as he can. He does not believe that he possibly can give true access to
the original" (1988: 111).

As a footnote to this debate, here is a formula that deserves to be tried: a short song can be performed twice, in the SL and then the TL. In Edinburgh, for example, a French song can be performed first in French – to people who know French imperfectly or not at all – and then in English. Their experience of the two versions will not be the same!

Translations for future music

One phenomenon that is far from rare is the *translated text that is subsequently set to music in the TL.* The composer Hugo Wolf used many German translations made from Italian or Spanish. Schubert even took some from Scots English. In some other cases a verse-translation done without no musical intention (e.g. of an Italian sonnet by Petrarca) is later selected by a musician and made into a song. This is especially common in sacred music: psalm-settings use translations out of Hebrew, musical versions of the Latin "Magnificat" use Jerome's translation from the Greek.

In some cases a translator may devise a text deliberately for subsequent musical setting – for example a Spanish translation of a Shakespeare song for which a Chilean composer will make new music for a new production. That translation should be different from a literary translation for a Shakespeare publication in Spanish, because it is a song-lyric for a future song-setting. The translator would find it easier to translate for future music than to devise a Spanish TT to fit pre-existing music, such as the Shakespeare music of Thomas Arne.

The making of translations for this purpose is slightly different from the "programme text" *skopos* discussed in chapter 3, because you are trying to produce an oral text, indeed a song-lyric in the TL. Sound and rhythm matter, and you may well choose to use some rhyme. These are matters for the next chapter.

Exercise (A) – A lyric that has lost its music

The following is a written prose translation of a lyric – a song with lyre accompaniment – by Sappho. It is about 2,600 years old, which explains the loss of its music. Try to rework it, in English or another TL, in order to make it suitable for musical setting. This means giving it a singable oral character, with phonic and rhythmic patterns, possibly including rhyme and repetition.

The moon has set, and the Pleiades too. It is midnight, time is passing, and I sleep alone.

Exercise (B) – Archaism

In an early translation of *Peer Gynt* (Ibsen/Grieg 1876 in an undated Victorian songbook) one finds this fragment of TT:

"But thou wilt come again, I know, and be mine.
The faithful word is spoken and I am always thine."

How could one justify the translator's use of archaic English? Here are some possible arguments:

1   The song is a prayer.
2   English people talked like that in 1876.
3   The drama is set in the distant past.
4   The Norwegian ST used unnatural, archaic language.
5   The character Solveig is a Quaker.
6   It achieves a good rhyme.

How many of those points are actually true? How many constitute good arguments for the use of "thou"? And how valid are any of these arguments in the twenty-first century?

Exercise (C) – A problematic phrase

The French phrase "mouches et papillons" (in a lyric by Bouilhet) would normally be rendered as (A) "flies and butterflies". But that creates a clumsy repetition of sound and meaning – "flies . . . flies" – not present in the ST. The phrase (B) "bees and butterflies" sounds better: perhaps the poet wished to write "abeilles" but needed a shorter word to fit in his line. Yet "bees" is semantically wrong for the line he actually wrote.

Would you opt for (A) or (B)? Or for something else?

To see the whole text: http://www.lieder.net/lieder/get_text.html?TextId=2927

Exercise (D) – Unnatural English

When two educated Christians in India encountered the following carol, they said: "This must be a translation, and a bad one too. No native speaker would write such poor English." What could have led them to this opinion? Here are the opening lines:

Away in a manger, no crib for a bed
The little Lord Jesus laid down his sweet head.
The cattle are lowing, the baby awakes.
But little Lord Jesus no crying he makes.

What evidence for their opinion can you find specifically in tense, rhyme, idiom, word-order, grammar and obscurity?

Further reading

Two good discussions of culture-specific items are:

Franco Aixelá, Javier (1996) "Culture-Specific Items in Translation", in Álvarez, Román & Carmen-África Vidal, M. (eds) *Translation, Power, Subversion*. Clevedon, Adelaide, Philadelphia, PA, Multilingual Matters, 52–78.

Pedersen, Jan (2011) *Subtitling Norms for Television: An Exploration Focussing on Extra-linguistic Cultural References*, Amsterdam, John Benjamins.

References

Flood, Joe (2015, November 13) Personal communication.

Golomb, Harai (2005) "Music-linked Translation (MLT) and Mozart's Operas" in Gorlée (1997).

Gorlée, Dinda (1997) "Intercode Translation: Words and Music in Opera" in *Target* 9/2: 235–270.

Graham, Arthur (1989) "A New Look at Recital Song Translation" in *Translation Review* 29: 31–37.

Gutt, Ernst-August (1991) "Translation as Interlingual Interpretive Use", in Venuti, Lawrence (ed) *The Translation Studies Reader*. London & New York, Routledge.

Nida, Eugene and Taber, C. (1969) *The Theory and Practice of Translation*, London & New York, Routledge.

Pountney, David (1975) Introduction to P. P. Fuchs (ed) *The Music Theatre of Walter Felsenstein*, New York, Norton.

Raffel, Burton (1988) *The Art of Translating Poetry*, Philadelphia, Pennsylvania State University.

Venuti, Lawrence (1995) *The Translator's Invisibility*, London & New York, Routledge.

Wagner, Richard (1893) *Richard Wagner's Prose Works* II, London, Kegan Paul (original in *Oper und Drama*, 1852).

Whitton, Kenneth (1984) *Lieder, an Introduction to German Song*, London, MacRae.

5 Singable translations (A) – like a pentathlon

Multiple constraints

Singable translations differ considerably from other kinds. On top of the normal considerations of meaning and naturalness, they require careful attention to ease of articulation, rhythm and often rhyme. These additional problems are created by the pre-existing music. In a singable translation the original melody, the tune which fitted the original words, will be re-used, virtually unchanged, but will be carrying different words – words in the TL largely derived from the ST. In many cases the music was composed with the ST as its starting-point, and so in a sense the translator has to work in the opposite direction, proceeding from the music in search of TL words.

The biggest challenge here is probably rhythm: you cannot ignore the stresses, the varying note-lengths or the syllabic patterns of the pre-existing music. Rhythm will be the main focus of chapter 6. Often translators choose to maintain the same syllable-count as the ST and a similar frequency of rhyming. But these are serious constraints, very unusual requirements for translators! Indeed, this set of constraints may be compared with the spatial limitations of subtitling wordy films or of translating from Japanese or Chinese into cramped websites or cartoon frames.

A disclaimer is made here: this book does not contend that songs *ought to be* performed in the language of the audience: that is a matter of debate (see the section in chapter 4). These chapters are intended for people who – for whatever reason – have decided to make a singable TT, and who would like strategies and tips on how to proceed with this difficult translating task.

Four tips

- Start with the key phrase. Don't automatically start at the beginning. The key phrase could be the line most often repeated, or the key phrase of the refrain – "smoke gets in your eyes", for example, or "the music of the night". That phrase may be the first line, of course, and that's fine. But if the last line is particularly punchy, then start your translating there . . . so as to ensure that the lyric leads up to something strong. Your version of that key phrase needs to be convincing: indeed it may make or break your translation. Hence the value of attending to it first and then fitting the surrounding lines to it (not vice versa).

- Identify the crucial parts of the text.
- Decide your priorities for this song – not just this songwriter or this style, but *this particular song*. Do you most want to achieve good rhythm, long vowels, legato phrasing or what?
- Decide whether or not you will use rhymes (and if so, give early attention to rhyming-words).

"Never in a work of art is everything equally significant" (Golomb 2005: 136).

The features of the text which you have not prioritised will probably not be well transferred. That is common in translating generally, and especially common when you translate, as here, under multiple constraints – not simply the normal need for accurate sense and natural style. This is all the more reason to be very clear about your strategy and objectives. Clarity will help you make good choices.

A pentathlon?

Most of the considerations can be summed up under five headings:

1) Singability; 2) sense; 3) naturalness; 4) rhythm; and 5) rhyme

These criteria are so dissimilar that some have been led to speak of a "juggling act". The metaphor proposed here is the "Pentathlon": this image likens the five criteria to the five events in which athletes must compete to maximise their points, events as different as a shot-put and a 100-metre sprint.

1   Singability
The criterion of *Singability* is judged by the phonetic suitability of the TT for singing, with reference to the physical organs involved in singing – the mouth, throat, lungs and vocal folds.
This is best assessed by singers who usually sing in the TL.

2   Sense
The criterion of *Sense* is judged by comparing the TT to the ST: is the meaning well transferred?
This is best assessed by truly bilingual people.

3   Naturalness
The criterion of *Naturalness* is judged within the SL: how natural is the style of the TT?
This is best assessed by native speakers of the TL.

4   Rhythm
The criterion of *Rhythm* is judged with reference to the music: how well does it fit?
This is best assessed by people with a good sense of rhythm: drummers, dancers etc.

5   Rhyme
The criterion of *Rhyme* focuses on a specific formal feature of the TT, the sounds of the line-endings. Rhymes typically match final vowel and preceding consonant

or final consonant and preceding vowel. How well does the TT rhyming match
the rhyming found in the ST?
This is the easiest criterion to assess, and usually the least important.

These five considerations can help guide translators in improving their TTs. They
can also be used to help evaluate the quality of singable translations and have
indeed been used for this purpose (Ó Luasa 2014). The sporting metaphor of the
pentathlon implies that the objective is a *high aggregate score across all these five
events*. Trade-offs are very likely to be required. Over-emphasis on Rhyme, for
example, compromises Sense.

One important question here is "Are the words of this song very important?"
There is a polarity between logocentric and musico-centric songs, as explained
in chapter 1 – with a "middle ground" for songs where words and music are
both very important. The genre of jazz song, for example, contains songs which
vary widely in this respect. These differences between individual songs point to
differing "pentathlon strategies". Thus, when you judge a particular song to be
musico-centric, you will tend to choose options that score highly on singability
even at the expense of sense. In logocentric songs you will tend to favour sense
over singability or rhythm. But discussion of specific examples is probably more
useful than further generalisation.

To negotiate the necessary trade-offs calls for greater flexibility than is needed
in other translating. For ordinary translating you already have a "toolbox" of
techniques – literal translation, paraphrase, transposition of parts of speech,
changes in word-order. But to make translations for singing you need to be not
only a translator of the SL but also a juggler of the TL. You should supplement
your normal toolbox with a "box of tricks", such as these:

*   *modulation* (for example the switch of perspective when you translate
    "Remember" as "Don't forget!")
*   *compensation in place* (inserting a detail in a different line of the TT because
    you couldn't fit it in the same line)
*   *generalisation* (superordinate words, such as "birds" for "robins")
*   *particularisation* (subordinate words, such as "toes" for "feet")
*   *near-synonyms*, (adjacent terms, such as "hares" for "rabbits")
*   *substitute metaphors*
*   *dilution* (reducing the number or complexity of items)
*   *repackaging*
*   *condensation*
*   *changing the kind of utterance.*

That last point means replacing one kind of utterance – a statement, exclamation,
question or imperative – with another. For example where a German hymn began
with an imperative *Nun danket alle . . .* the translator instead delivered a statement: "Now thank we all . . .." Or where a romantic song by Liszt began with a
repeated imperative: "O lieb', o lieb', so lang du lieben kannst" (Freiligrath), the

French translator substituted an exclamation *Amour, amour, trésor béni de Dieu*, even though *amour* is not a verb at all.

These techniques are relatively abnormal in ordinary translation, since they do not transfer meaning perfectly. But they are good to call on, when you have strong reasons, and when you have exhausted your other options. To take a simple example, the German preposition *vor* means "in front of", yet if your song requires a monosyllable you may well translate it with the less precise word "near". In terms of the pentathlon metaphor, you would justify this unusual solution by saying that "despite being sub-optimal, this gives a higher score overall". Or to take a metaphor from archery: you don't need to hit the bull's-eye, you do have to hit the board.

Singability – Relative singability in physical and phonetic terms

The term **"Singability"** is used here to mean *relative ease of vocalisation*. Ease is achieved by meeting the demands of articulation, breath, dynamics and resonance in the physical action of singing. Hence this first criterion is *physical and phonetic*, and for translators it affects the choice of vowels and consonants. In this sense, Singability is something that professional singers and singing-teachers are best placed to evaluate, because they understand the physical challenges that can be found in the words and music of the song, the challenges of articulation, breathing, dynamics and resonance. The ideal translation, according to one singer, will "have the same mouth-feel" as the original: there will be "matching of long

---

Dogmas about singable translations

These are fixed ideas some people have. While some are not without value, you need to take them all with a grain of salt – otherwise they can be poisonous!

Translate line by line, starting at the beginning.
Retain the original vowel-sound of any long note.
The sense must be transferred at all costs.
All ST metaphors must be retained.
All repetition must be retained.
Resort to archaic language as often as you wish.
Never alter punctuation or shift commas.
Never change the number of syllables in a phrase.
The TT needs to rhyme as frequently as the ST.
The rhyme-scheme of the original must be kept.
Imperfect rhymes are never acceptable.
No change, however slight, may be made to the tune of the song.

"The perfect is the enemy of the good" – attributed to Voltaire.

---

vowels to long vowels, short vowels to short, single consonants to single consonants." You can't expect Google Translate to deliver that!

What we are seeking, then, is a version *which the singer who will sing it deems singable* – a contingent and pragmatic formula. To state the converse, any TT that scores poorly on this criterion is a failure and will not be sung or even pronounced, whatever its other virtues may be. That is why it is listed here as the first criterion.

Relative ease of vocalisation requires the avoidance of tongue-twisters. Most people, admittedly, can pronounce tongue-twisters in their own language, and Czech singers can probably sing "strč prst skrz krk" at a medium tempo. But translators need to avoid creating problems of this kind. What if the source phrase itself is hard to articulate? These cases are fairly rare (except in rap music), and when they occur they may be deliberate. One line in *My Fair Lady* (Lerner/Loewe) – "Anyone who's ever been in love will tell you that!" – squeezes 12 syllables (and more than 12 consonants) into one measure of moderate waltz time – nearly 5 syllables per second! This is an unusual special effect, and one would expect a translation of it to use fewer syllables, though without destroying the effect.

Here are four tips for Singability:

1   *Try to have open-ended syllables.* Syllables consisting of consonant-vowel (CV, as in "go") are better than those with a consonant at the end (VC or CVC, as in "out" or "bout"). This is easy enough in some languages, such as Italian, Japanese, Finnish and Maori. Those languages most dominated by consonants are less intrinsically singable (Serbian or Polish, for example), and yet song-lyrics and song-translations are found in all. Translators of songs into English sometimes have difficulty finding good open syllables.

   One very bad case of a CVC syllable occurs at the end of Liszt's song "O quand je dors", on the word "Laura". The final syllable RA is given a long high F# – a good ten seconds long – difficult enough in the original French with its open syllable. Yet an old publication from Kahnt Verlag prints "singable" versions in English and German which assign that note to the words "night" and "Nacht" – thus expecting the singer to pronounce a T at the very end. If you can't avoid ending a long syllable with a consonant, you'd better make it N or L, because these don't automatically close the jaw. It is said that some singers omit all consonants on high notes; it is certain that audiences can find it too hard to hear any – and that this can affect understanding of the words.

2   *Avoid consonant clusters.* A phrase with more than two consonants per syllable is less singable than one where every syllable is a regular CV (one consonant followed by one vowel). Thus a good songwriter in English will avoid the word "respectful", will change the word "whilst" into "while", will amend "prospects" to "chances", will reject the phrase "much better" in favour of "far better" and may revise the cliché "the cold light of day" to "the cool light of day".

Some relativity is needed here, however. Many Russian singers have successfully articulated Tchaikovsky's *Niet tol'ko tot kto znal*, despite its abundance of plosive

How long is the note? How fast is the music?

Standard notation can tell you. This chart gives the main symbols for
note-values (= relative lengths):

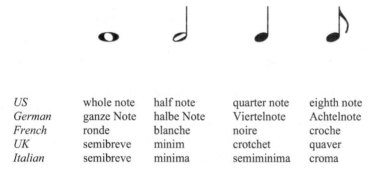

US	whole note	half note	quarter note	eighth note
German	ganze Note	halbe Note	Viertelnote	Achtelnote
French	ronde	blanche	noire	croche
UK	semibreve	minim	crotchet	quaver
Italian	semibreve	minima	semiminima	croma

The US and German terms tell us the fractions, while the French terms
neatly describe the symbols. Most of the British terms are actually
misnomers (the longer notes are called minimal and semi-brief, while the
word 'crotchet' denotes a symbol with no hook!).

It would be nice if the ♩ was always 1 second long, but really it varies
from about 0.4 to 1.2 seconds, according to tempo. The "time-signature"
gives an indication of that. Traditional Italian terms range from slow to
quick, usually in this order:
   Lento, Largo, Adagio, Andante, Moderato, Allegro, Vivace, Presto

A metronome indication, when provided, is much more precise:
♩ = 70 means 70 per minute, a steady pulse-rate. But you sometimes see
♩ = 140, and many performers will go slower or faster, or will vary the
tempo.

Figure 5.1 "How long is the note?"

consonants. Yet it would be hard for Italian singers to perform this song in Russian (or in German: the composer actually set a translation of the Goethe poem "Nur wer die Sehnsucht kennt"). Italian singers have difficulty enough with a line from *My Fair Lady* – "I have often walk'd down this street" – with its cluster of plosives KDD. A group of four consonants makes a tongue-twister and should be rejected, especially if they include plosives. The Dutch translator Marlieke Gevaerts explicitly avoided the word "zachtheid" as being hard to sing (2012: 24).

3   *Be sparing with plosive consonants.* These six – TDPBKG – cause the tongue or lips to stop the air-flow, and can pose particular problems at the end of syllables. Consonants like M and R give fewer problems than S, Z, F and V. It is particularly desirable for smooth flowing passages in a song to be translated with what could be called "legato-friendly phonemes". But sometimes the converse is needed: some songs deliberately exploit plosive effects for staccato passages, or for snappy rhymes (e.g. Barbier's rhymes ending -AK in the prelude to Offenbach's *Contes d'Hoffmann*). Such staccato effects may be hard to replicate in languages that have few closed syllables, such as Japanese.

4   *Pay close attention to vowels.* Singers work hard to balance the need for clear and accurate text delivery with their wish to achieve an even and resonant sound throughout their range. It is helpful if the translator has some knowledge of what aids resonance and what reduces it, in order to devise the most easy-to-sing option when there is a choice.

Most classically trained singers are taught to use the Italian vowels [i: e: a: o: u:] as a model for clear, resonant vowel sound. These are described as "pure" vowels. Whatever they are singing, they will typically try to get as close to one of these vowels as possible, while still conveying the meaning of the words. Some vowels are intrinsically longer than others, and the International Phonetic Alphabet indicates this by the symbol [:]. Conversely, some are intrinsically short, like the vowel in the English "bit". This affects singing greatly: to sing a short vowel on a long note is technically difficult, singers will naturally distort it, gravitating to the equivalent long vowel, and perhaps unintentionally producing a different word.

There is also an important distinction between front or closed vowels and back or open vowels. Front vowels, such as [i:] and [e:], are formed with a closed mouth and high tongue, forward in the mouth. Back or open vowels, such as [a:], are formed with the tongue hump lower, and are felt further back in the mouth. The vowel [u:] has a low tongue but is forward in the mouth, so is considered a closed vowel. Thus there are front (closed) vowels in the following English words: *bat, bait, beet, bet, bit, boot* and *but.* And there are back (open) vowels in the words *boat, bot, bout* and *bought.* Most languages have a similar range of vowels, though no two are identical. See Figure 5.2 for English vowels.

Although there is no such thing as a good or bad vowel, closed vowels are harder to sing on high pitches, and open vowels can sometimes be harder to sing on low notes. In musical notation we can define high notes as those near, on or

Approximate position of vowels in English, by highest point of tongue
(excluding diphthongs, where the tongue moves)

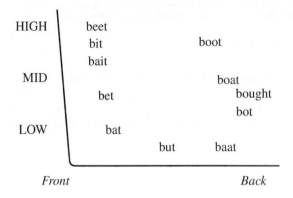

Figure 5.2 Mouth diagram "bit/but" etc.

above the top of the five-line stave. Yet what is felt as a high pitch varies by voice type: anything above a D needs to be thought about carefully. If you know it's for a tenor or soprano, anything on an E or F is on his or her break and might be modified; and any high note above F could be unrecognizable, no matter what the language. In order to create more space in the mouth to produce a resonant sound, the singer will move closed vowels towards more open ones at the top of his or her range: for instance [i:] becomes [e:] and at times even [a:] so that the sound is not strangled. If the translator can choose words with open vowels on high notes, that will be helpful to the singer.

Short vowels can pose a challenge at any point in the singer's range, not just the extremes: the singer will move a short vowel towards the nearest long vowel to achieve a resonant sound. In French the neutral E found in "je" should not be placed on a downbeat or a long note. In English and German one of the most problematic vowels to sing is the [i] as in "bin", which will be lengthened to an [i:], with the possibility of distorting the meaning if placed on a long note ("bin" becomes "been"). The vowel in words like "but" will be modified by the singer to something close to [a:], and so can sound peculiar if you place it on a long note – or a melisma of short notes (which would pose the same problem). The weak neutral vowel heard in the most common English word "the" should be reserved for short weak notes (or replaced with another determiner such as "these" or "my"). The English word "love" can be especially difficult, yet it appears fairly often in song-lyrics! If you're translating the German *Liebe*, for example sung on a long, melismatic phrase, then avoid the English "love", because it readily turns into "lurve" (and that sound is best reserved for Elvis impersonators).

These points about vowels were not realised by the translator of one fine French song. Here (Figure 5.3) are the first words of "Les Berceaux" (Sully-Prudhomme/

Figure 5.3 The Stately Ships (Fauré), score fragment

Gabriel Fauré), in an old publication (c1900) that prints a translation supposedly for singing in English. The tempo is rather slow (*andante*), with the result that the word "ships" must be held for about 2 seconds – too long, surely, for that English vowel. Even worse, the first word "the" is placed on a downbeat and a longish note (at least 1 second). To do this on the French article *le* was unusual but acceptable; to do it in English was incompetent. No wonder hardly anyone actually sang this TT.

A Chabrier song from the same period concerns *les cochons roses* and puts a melisma of seven notes on the open [o] vowel of "roses". That one syllable needs to last 3 seconds, which ruled out translating with the obvious English words "pink" and "pigs", since those have front closed vowels. One translator cheated and left the phrase in French.

Untrained singers, who may not have mastered the art of even resonance across their range, are particularly vulnerable to the difficulties discussed above, so the take-away points for the translator are:

• Use words containing pure, Italian vowels where possible.
• Avoid the use of short vowels on long notes.
• Be aware of pitch and avoid placing hard-to-sing words on high notes.

The ideal here is to create a TT that is as easy to sing as the ST.

In every existing song, either the composer setting the text already knew the sounds of the words (working music-first) or else the lyricist already knew where the high and low notes would be. When the Beatles wrote the lyric known as "Yesterday", they first had the tune and they then chose excellent words for long notes: "play", "game", "be", "go", "know" and "say". Translators don't have the luxury of open choice, but should at least be aware of which sounds are sure to work well.

The above discussion uses a narrow sense of the term "Singability": it excludes the non-phonetic considerations covered by the other four terms. Some other people use the term more broadly, for example singers may call a phrase "unsingable" on rhythmic grounds or on grounds of unnatural style or register. In Johan Franzon's discussions of singability (2005 & 2008) he covers the above points, but includes other things like rhythm, rhyme and how well it expresses meaning – important matters which are discussed here under other rubrics.

With regard to phonetic matters, some translators try to go further and to place an important long note not only on a long singable vowel but on *the same vowel*, thus replicating some of the precise sounds of the ST at the same point of the phrase. This is often impossible – and it is certainly not essential: the important thing is for the TT vowel to be one of the readily singable ones. If a singer tells you: "This melisma is on a long Italian A, give me the same vowel please in English", you should ask for two or three acceptable alternatives. Even key words can be translated with a different vowel from the ST, but it does need to be suitable and usable.

Sense – Semantic accuracy

The term **"Sense"** denotes the semantic matters that dominate discussions of non-fiction translating: *meaning, content and intent.* These matters were discussed in chapter 2, which stressed the need for a TT to convey a song's meaning without omission, change or addition. Sense is badly handled whenever a TT acquires a different verbal meaning from the ST. The translator who rendered "The answer is blowin' in the wind" as *Écoute la réponse dans le vent* ("Listen to the answer in the wind") omitted the verb "blow", added the verb "écouter" and changed a statement into an imperative. That line does not score very highly on Sense. But how much does that matter?

Perhaps not too much. For this chapter, which concerns TTs intended for singing, lexical fidelity is often undesirable, and perhaps even, as Burton Raffel puts it, is "not only not expected, not only impossible of attainment, but in fact counterproductive" (1988: 146). The reason why it is undesirable is that it reduces flexibility and underplays the need for Naturalness. For such translations, therefore, sense may be acceptably transferred through choices which are imprecise, such as near-synonyms, superordinates etc.). Here are some examples:

> *"apprehension" amended to "fear" – near-synonym*
> *"banana" amended to "fruit" – superordinate*
> *"tree" amended to "poplar" – subordinate*
> *"apple" amended to "pear" – adjacent item in same category*

In normal informative translating, such choices would be unacceptable. Yet they are desirable here whenever they help the overall "pentathlon score". This does not mean awarding 10/10 for a line that translates an apple as a pear. But it does mean that the penalty for that inaccuracy can be outweighed by a better score on another criterion. (For example one might choose "pear" for its rhyme, or to save one syllable.) In making singable translations, you need to widen your notion of a "synonym", and you may choose not a normal dictionary but a more accommodating word-list such as a thesaurus. One translator confronting the unambiguous number 120 turned it into 99, for the sake of a rhyme, judging that 99 was imperfect but "close enough". For most texts it would be a disgraceful error, but not in a song.

Those making singable translations into tonal languages – Chinese, Vietnamese – must also watch the effect of pitch on meaning: a word that is perfect in a written TT or when sung on a low note may have the wrong meaning on a high note.

When translators score very poorly on this criterion of sense – whether by incompetence or strategic choice – the TT should more accurately be called an adaptation. One might even say that these translators are "opting out" of the pentathlon (for reasons which may be good or bad).

If then some of them may claim that they were "forced out", be sceptical: many singable translations score quite well on sense. A 1945 publication of the Gershwin song "The Man I Love" prints two translations – along with the ST – between the musical staves. Thus at the start of the refrain we read under the notes:

Someday he'll come along	*The man I love*
Il me viendra un jour	*Mon seul amour*
Un día llegará	*mi gran amor*

These French and Spanish versions are close translations, and score well on most other criteria. Adaptation will be discussed later in chapter 7.

Naturalness – Convincing style and register

The term **"Naturalness"** assumes that the TT will be natural in the sense of being *a text that could have been created spontaneously in the TL* – by a songwriter, poet or other wordsmith within the target culture. To consider this criterion is part of a common translating principle: *Observe the norms of the TL.*

This matter has been discussed in chapter 4, notably in the section about avoiding rare words, but is more delicate when the TT is to be sung. Translations which sound translated – sometimes called "overt" translations – do not work properly in performance. Singers find it difficult to put across an unnatural text, for example one with inverted word-order (whether produced for the sake of rhyme or for some false fidelity to the ST). And audiences have difficulties listening, since unnaturalness demands an additional processing effort. A TT is not worth making unless it can be understood while the song is sung.

In a sense the translator needs to deceive: you need to give the false impression that your TT was the original text, and even – ideally – that it predated the music. As one translator once put it: "The target text must sound as if the music had been fitted to it, even though it was actually composed to fit the source text" (Dyer-Bennett 1965: 292). So this criterion is a stylistic one: it concerns *style in the TL*. The opposite of naturalness is clumsiness and klunkiness. For example a TT using a word like "albeit" or "acrimonious" might be rejected by an English-speaking singer who says: "That's not a word that can be sung with sincerity" or "That phrase doesn't ring true. It's too awkward." If other singers agree, you must count that stylistic objection as valid and should find a more natural alternative.

Although some scholars, not without reason, have spoken of making a TT sound "naturally" in terms of rhythms and stress-patterns being "unnatural" (Golomb 2005: 124), those matters are discussed below under the rubric Rhythm, which begins the next chapter.

A good example of a singable translation

The song printed here, "Le Fossoyeur", by a major songwriter from southern France, has been translated. Both texts are reproduced here with permission.

"LE FOSSOYEUR"
code œuvre : WW002474754
Paroles et Musique de Georges Brassens
© Warner Chappell Music France – 1952

Dieu sait qu' je n'ai pas le fond méchant,
Qu' je ne souhait' jamais la mort des gens;
Mais si l'on ne mourait plus,
J' crèv'rais d' faim sur mon talus . . .
J' suis un pauvre fossoyeur.

Les vivants croient que j' n'ai pas d' remords
A gagner mon pain sur l' dos des morts;
Mais ça m' tracasse et d'ailleurs.
J' les enterre à contre-cœur . . .
J' suis un pauvre fossoyeur.

J'ai beau m' dir' que rien n'est éternel,
J' peux pas trouver ça tout naturel;
Et jamais je ne parviens
A prendr' la mort comme ell' vient . . .
J'suis un pauvre fossoyeur.

Et plus j' lâch' la bride à mon émoi.
Et plus les copains s'amus'nt de moi;
I' m' dis'nt: "Mon vieux par moments
T'as un' figur' d'enterr'ment . . ."
J' suis un pauvre fossoyeur.

Ni vu ni connu, brav' mort adieu!
Si du fond d' la terre on voit l' bon Dieu.
Dis-lui l' mal que m'a coûté
La dernière pelletée.
J' suis un pauvre fossoyeur.
J' suis un pauvre fossoyeur.

The Gravedigger
Singable translation by Joe Flood

Lord knows I'm not one who'd ever pray
That another's soul be borne away
But if death stopped coming 'round

I would starve here on this mound
A poor gravedigger am I

There are those who think that I take pride
In a living made off those who've died
But look closely and you'll see
I don't do it willingly
A poor gravedigger am I

Any time I set my feelings free
That's the time my friends make fun of me
They all poke me in the side
Say, "You look like someone died!"
A poor gravedigger am I

"Death's just part of life," I hear them say,
But I don't know why it is that way
There are some, but I'm not one,
Who can take death as it comes
A poor gravedigger am I

Dear departed one who I'll never know
Should you meet the Lord six feet below
Let him know how much it hurt
This last shovelful of dirt
A poor gravedigger am I
Your poor gravedigger am I

PROSE TRANSLATION for those who don't read French:

> *God knows I don't have a bad core, that I don't want the death of people;
> but if dying stopped happening I'd starve to death on my mound . . . I'm a
> poor gravedigger.*

> *The living think I have no remorse in earning my bread on the back of the
> dead; but that bothers me, and besides, I bury them unwillingly . . . I'm a
> poor gravedigger.*

> *However much I say that nothing lasts forever, I can't find that totally natural;
> and I never manage to just take death as she comes . . . I'm a poor gravedigger.*

> *The more I give free rein to my feelings, the more my mates make fun of me;
> they say: "Old chap, sometimes you have a funeral face" . . . I'm a poor
> gravedigger.*

Noticed by no one, goodbye good dead man! If down in the earth you see the good Lord, tell him what pain it caused me, that last shovelful . . . I'm a poor gravedigger. I'm a poor gravedigger.

The Brassens original can be heard on https://www.youtube.com/results?search_query=le+fossoyeur+brassens

The Joe Flood version on http://joeflood.bandcamp.com/album/joe-flood-translates-and-sings-georges-brassens

THE SOURCE-TEXT. In print, Brassens spells many words with elisions, placing an apostrophe where standard written French has an E, and where some singers would have sounded a weak syllable. This reflects conversational pronunciation. It also enables him to tweak the rhythm: for example he chooses whether or not to pronounce a syllable on "le".

This is a strophic song. Note the consistent rhythmic pattern (with lines 1 and 2 longer than 3, 4 and 5). It fits the music perfectly, even down to the pause after syllable 5 of each verse. Note the consistent rhyme-scheme. Note also that "Je" does not mean Brassens himself, but a fictional character expressing particular views.

THE ENGLISH VERSION. Unlike the over-literal prose translation, Joe Flood's version has given attention to singability, sense, naturalness, rhythm and rhyme. He spent a long time on this and has this to say: "A version of Brassens that doesn't at least aspire to his kind of craftsmanship could never give the listener even a glimpse of his genius." Of the gravedigger in this song he says: "I wanted to present the character with both sympathy and humor." As for the rhyming of verse four, which does not match the ST: "It bothered me to rhyme 'one' with 'comes' because I had managed to find exact rhymes for every other couplet in the song, but I felt that the internal rhyming word 'some' helped to draw the ear away from the imperfection."

What if you find faults with this TT? Well, singable translations can easily be criticised on some ground or other. Almost as easily, alternative phrases can be suggested which score better on one criterion. Yet such suggestions can infuriate translators, who already know that most of their lines could be "corrected" in at least one respect. What the pentathlon approach requires, however, is that *for any proposed amendment to constitute a genuine improvement, it must increase the overall aggregate* calculated on all five criteria. An amendment that fails to do this has limited value, and may well lead to a reduction in the total "pentathlon score" – that is a key point of this whole argument.

Some trade-offs and compromises are really difficult. The Dutch translator of "Le Métèque" by Georges Moustaki notes ruefully: "A big semantic loss. The notion of 'Wandering Jew' is in our language *wandelende jood*. But we failed to find a way of incorporating that into our translation without major losses in rhythm and singability. So we sacrificed it for the sake of a singable rhythmic text" (Gevaerts 2012: 41). That sacrifice was pragmatically justified.

Harai Golomb puts the strong case for compromise in these words: "Semantic approximations and loose summaries, that would be hair-raising in music-free contexts and normally rejected as translational non-starters, can be accommodated [in singable translations], especially if sacrifices of this type earn the text such valued qualities as rhythmical elegance, witty and effective word-music alignment, and immediate communicability" (2005: 133).

***

Exercise (A)

The following lines come from an Anti-Smoking Rap:

> If you think it's cool, if you think it's smart
> then you're 'bout as cool as a helephant's fart

Not all details of this couplet are equally important. There is meaning, rhyme, rhythm, humour, simile, non-standard language, vulgarity etc. If you were to translate it, what elements would you prioritise?

Exercise (B) – Consonants

Look at the incidence of consonant clusters in the languages you know.

How often are two consonants together? Is there sometimes a cluster of three consonants? Or even more? Are these easy to pronounce? Do they include the ZDR cluster, which exists in Russian?

Now consider the songs you know in these languages: do these songs include words like "strict" (English and French) with two consonant clusters close together? Do singers in performance omit some consonants? Does this affect intelligibility?

Exercise (C) – Vowels

You can't do this exercise without making a noise!

Try singing these open-ended syllables, on a rising scale:

BEE BEE BEE BEE BEE
BOO BOO BOO BOO BOO
BAA BAA BAA BAA BAA
Are they equally easy to sing?
Are any of them hard to sing on a low note?
Which is the best for a long high note?

Now try singing the same vowels with a consonant at the end:

BEET BEET BEET BEET BEET
BOOT BOOT BOOT BOOT BOOT

BART BART BART BART BART
Does the final T make a difference?
Does it make a difference if you sound or don't sound that R in BART?
Which is the easiest to sing?

Here is a list of thirteen English words containing most of the vowels and diphthongs in the language:

BAT BAIT BART BET BEAT BERT BIT BOT BOAT BOOT BOUT
BOUGHT BUT

They do not, of course, all feel the same to sing. Which ones open your jaw the most? Which ones hold your jaw fairly closed? Which ones permit your lips to open wide?

For a long high note, which vowels would make the singer's task easier? What about the other languages you know? How many vowels do they use? Which vowels open the jaws most? Which pose the most problems for singing?

Further reading

This chapter and the next rework with greater precision two earlier articles: Low, Peter (2003) "Singable Translations of Songs" *Perspectives* 11/2: 87–103 and Low, Peter (2005) "The Pentathlon Approach to Translating Songs" in Gorlée (2005).

Also recommended on singable translations are:

Apter, Ronnie & Herman, Mark (2016) *Translating for Singing – the Theory, Art and Craft of Translating Lyrics*, London, Bloomsbury.

The articles by Franzon and Golomb in Gorlée, Dinda (ed) (2005) *Song and Significance: Virtues and Vices of Vocal Translation*, Amsterdam & New York, Rodopi.

Franzon, Johan (2008) "Choices of Song Translation. Singability in Print, Subtitles and Sung Performance" *The Translator* 14/2: 373–399.

Kelly, Andrew (1987) "Translating French Song as a Language Learning Activity" in *British Journal of Language Teaching* and reprinted in *Traduire et interpréter Georges Brassens*, 91–112.

Traduire et interpréter Georges Brassens (1992–1993), a collective volume from the Institut Supérieur de Traducteurs et Interprètes, Bruxelles.

Drinker, Henry (1952) "On Translating Vocal Texts" in *The Musical Quarterly*, 225–240.

Strangways, A.H.F. (1921) "Song-Translating" in *Music and Letters*, 1921: 211–224.

References

Dyer-Bennett, Richard (1965) Preface to Schubert, *The Lovely Milleress*, New York, Schirmer, quoted in Emmons, Shirley (1979) *The Art of the Song Recital*, New York, Schirmer.

Franzon, Johan (2005) "Musical Comedy Translation" in Gorlée (2005).

Franzon, Johan (2008) "Choices in Song Translation" in *The Translator* 14/2: 373–399.

Gevaerts, Marlieke (2012) "Traduire le Métèque" unpublished thesis, Utrecht University.

Golomb, Harai (2005) "Music-linked Translation (MLT) and Mozart's Operas" in Gorlée (2005).

Gorlée, Dinda (ed) (2005) *Song and Significance: Virtues and Vices of Vocal Translation*, Amsterdam & New York, Rodopi.

Ó Luasa, Seán (2014) "Case Study: A Survey and Translation Quality Assessment of Popular Music Translated" unpublished thesis, Dublin City University.

Raffel, Burton (1988) *The Art of Translating Poetry*, Philadelphia, Pennsylvania State University.

6   Singable translations (B) – rhythm and rhyme

Tackling the problems of rhythm

What matters here is *the rhythm of the music.* This is usually easy to feel. It is not the rhythm of the spoken words; it is that of the pre-existing music with its down-beats, bar-lines and note-lengths. A good TT will match these musical rhythms. The translator's duty to the composer requires a high degree of respect for this pre-existing musical rhythm.

The rhythm of the music is not the same as poetic rhythm, often codified as tetrameter, *alexandrin, octosíllabo* etc. Consider the opening of the "Marseillaise":

> Allons enfants de la patrie,
> Le jour de gloire est arrivé

If this were a poem, we would identify the rhythm as two *octosyllabes*, a common poetic metre in French. But no, this is a song-lyric, and it has some syllables that are much stronger than others, something like this:

> Allons en-|FANTS de la pa-|TRI- i – e
> Le jour de |GLOI-re est arri-|VÉ

The first line has ten musical notes, not eight. Those vertical strokes are bar-lines followed immediately by downbeats. We could even notate the rhythms to distinguish strong for weak:

- - -/- - -/- - - - - -/- - -/

Here the slash / denotes a strong syllable. Furthermore, the notes of the tune vary significantly in length, from about 0.3 seconds to 2.4. So what a translator would really have to match is this vocal line (Figure 6.1). Fortunately this blood-thirsty marching-song does not need translating.

In singable translating you are seeking also a match for the note-values of the music. You must therefore pay attention to the length of vowels – as indicated above in the section on "singability" – without ignoring the role of consonants either. In some cases you must also take account of rests. For example a line

Figure 6.1 Allons enfants (Marseillaise)

which on paper looks unbroken may in music contain a significant rest – and you have to prevent this gap from coming in the middle of a word.

Consider this line from the Beatles: "We all live in a yellow submarine". To fit the music perfectly, you would need to seek 10 syllables with stresses on 1, 3, 6 and 10. Furthermore, the last 5 syllables would need to be separable, because they are then repeated as "yellow submarine, yellow submarine". In terms of rhythm, the objective is clear. But a perfect match might be achievable only at great cost to another criterion.

Downbeats matter more than syllable-count

The opposite of a perfect match is a non-match. That problem is very common: indeed translations which were not made deliberately to fit existing music – those mentioned earlier in this book – almost never fit. Even when a line of the TT has the same syllable-count as the ST, its accents often fall on inappropriate words, such as articles or short prepositions.

In some cases your first draft may have too few syllables. What do you do then? One option may be to choose longer words, though this may conflict with the requirement of naturalness. Another option might be to add a new word or phrase, or repeat a word or phrase. These are real possibilities. But be careful: any words added should give the appearance of coming from the subtext of the source. For example the TT may have a monosyllabic noun where 3 syllables are wanted, and one can deftly precede this with a plausible, natural-sounding adjective that coheres with the overall feeling of the text without adding anything very striking. If, for example, the Japanese word for "insects" takes 6 syllables and 6 notes, you may try the option "butterflies and beetles" (subordinate words). Or if the ST describes water with a pentasyllabic adjective meaning "rough", you may need in English to say "perilous and rough".

Conversely, there may be times when your draft TT has too many syllables. Then you should try to condense the line, perhaps by omitting a short adjective.

To score 100 per cent for rhythm, you cannot add or subtract syllables. The pentathlon approach, however, encourages you to seek trade-offs with other criteria. You should therefore be wary about any rigid pieces of advice. For example these remarks by Judi Palmer:

> the number of syllables . . . must be identical to the number of syllables in the original – occasionally, some librettists may use additional notes, though this is considered bad practice as it alters more than one medium.

Tweaking syllables in English

Fewer syllables	more syllables	tweak tactic
A man	A young man	± *adjective*
There was	There once was	± *adverb*
I say she . . .	I say that she . . .	± *conjunction*
He can't	He cannot	± *elision*
A man	A fellow	*synonym*
Each	Every	*synonym*
Not	Never	*near-synonym*
Vow	Promise	*near-synonym*
Books	A book	*number*
I teach	He teaches	*person*
I teach	I'm teaching	*tense*
They end	They ended	*tense*
He missed	He misses	*tense*
She	Mary	*pronoun <—> name*

In other languages similar tweaks are available – though not always the same ones. In German one might add a tiny word like "doch" or "ja", or omit an unstressed vowel, shortening "Leben" if necessary to "Leb'n".

In French oral texts, many elisions are optional, and the negative "ne" can be omitted in informal styles.

Obviously, there are a number of constraints on the translator/librettist: not only must s/he attempt accurately to translate the original text, but also echo the sound of the original words, limiting the choice of vocabulary considerably.

(2012: 23–24)

Those are overstatements. Adding additional notes does indeed alter the musical medium, yet alterations of this kind are sometimes insignificant and therefore acceptable. Similarly "echoing the sound" is unduly limiting – a similar sound will usually be good enough. Besides, in strophic songs, where every musical phrase is repeated with different words, variation in both consonants and vowels existed already in the source.

Stress

Stress is determined either by the fixed stress on certain words or syllables or else by their position in a word-group. English has more rigid stress than many other languages. For example the word "hippopotamus" has to be stressed on the third syllable – not the fourth (which Flanders and Swann used to do, ridiculously). Musical setting often increases the difference between stressed and unstressed syllables. The translator needs to identify which syllables of the ST are stressed in the music and look to provide corresponding stressed syllables in the TL.

This problem is of course irrelevant to non-singable translations. Normally between English and French one translates "royal" as "royal" and "imagine" as "imagine" – options which are perfect semantically and etymologically (they are cognates). But for singing they don't work, because the stresses fall differently. At times you find a quick solution, like replacing a word with its synonym, for example "maybe" with "perhaps", "lessen" with "reduce", "request" with "ask for". This must be harder in those languages (Czech, Finnish?) which overwhelmingly stress the first syllable of words. At other times you struggle even with names and cognate words, even when the syllable count is the same. Downbeats matter more than syllable-count.

Note that you can't add punctuation to a singable translation: you are forced to adapt to the "punctuation" given by the music – and this may reduce your options. To take an extreme case, a song supposedly featuring a pickled-herring merchant may be subtly transformed by the rhythm so that it calls him a pickled herring-merchant.

There is a rhythmic mistake in the most famous of oratorios, *Messiah*, on the line "And the dead shall be rais'd incorruptible". Confronted with that long final word, the composer put a downbeat on its fourth syllable, producing an ending that sounds like "tibble" or "teeble". This was a forgivable mistake by the composer (a Saxon named Händel), who probably knew the Italian word *incorruttibile*, which stresses syllable four. In performance many singers choose to adjust the rhythm and/or melody in order to place the stress correctly on "rup", the third syllable.

Line-endings

Although song-lyrics often have lines ending in stressed syllables, this is far from universal. Even in English you often find lines ending in a two-syllable word like "offer" or "finish" where the final syllable is weak. In Spanish and Italian songs, for example, many lines end with an unstressed A or O; in French about half the final syllables end in a weak E (silent in speech, but often sounded in song). These line-endings – sometimes called feminine or trochaic endings – coincide with a similar ending to the musical phrase: the penultimate note has the downbeat, not the final note, which is relatively soft. This means that the translator needs to find a trochaic word (strong-weak) like "merry", preferably ending in a vowel. One of the languages where this can be difficult is English, given its relative lack of inflexions. If you are translating into English, you will find the -ing and -ly suffixes useful. A typical adjustment in English is to change "keen to come" into "keen on coming".

Sometimes you may be tempted to slur the two notes together, so that *Liebe* (2 syllables) becomes "Love". This is not ideal, but may sometimes prove the best solution available. Conversely, it is sometimes necessary to transform a stressed line-ending (e.g. "life") into 2 syllables sung at the same pitch, strong-weak (e.g. *vida* in Spanish). In some languages penultimate stress is the norm, and so one would expect songs translated from English into (say) Polish to turn some mono-syllabic endings into 2 syllables, strong-weak.

Prominent words

Perfect sequential alignment of TT to ST is desirable but not usually crucial. A tricky problem arises, however, when the rhythm and melody-line highlight particular words, not just by putting them on the downbeat, but by placing them at the crest of the phrase or by giving them a high-pitched climax. Such highlighted words – what Wagner's metaphor called "the musical ridge" – should ideally be translated at the same location, because otherwise the sequential focus of the line will be altered and the spotlight will fall on a different word. This is very apparent with comic punch-lines: the word that triggers the laughter is often located at the end of the phrase, and ought not to come earlier. But humour is not the only issue: this applies to any notable or surprising word.

This can be tricky enough when SL and TL use similar word-order (e.g. subject-verb-object). It must be a real headache when they don't, for example if you are translating Italian into Turkish. You will have to call on all the tools of creative problem-solving!

Short phrases

"In general", writes Johan Franzon, "the longer the musical lines, the easier it may be for translators to accommodate the syntax of their particular language" (2008: 387). Unfortunately, many songs contain short phrases, often with only 2 or 3 syllables. And the repetitive nature of songs may mean that these short phrases are repeated, sometimes separated by rests in the music. This is inflexible and annoying. It is seldom acceptable to make pauses in the middle of words or even within small word-groups. Even those who claim that all sentences are translatable never contend that all short phrases can be translated as short phrases. How can the original rhythm be retained?

This example (Figure 6.2) shows a successful solution. The German translator of Händel's *Messiah* was confronted with the words "Rejoice – rejoice – rejoice

Figure 6.2 Rejoice (Messiah)

greatly" including a five-note melisma on the third "-joice". Because the obvious German verb *frohlocken* ("to rejoice") has 3 syllables not 2, the translator cleverly inserted a credible 2-syllable verb and got this result. Nothing significant is lost there: the sense of "greatly" remains present in the subtext. And nothing unwanted is added, since "erwach" ("wake up") is quite appropriate. And although the TT now has one extra syllable, that is neatly accommodated by reducing the melisma from five to four notes. The resultant phrase sounds indeed as if the composer had begun with this German text, even though he in fact began with the English – which is itself a translation from Hebrew.

What of the short phrase "Show me", in the musical *My Fair Lady*? In Johan Franzon's fine study (2005) of various translations, he concluded rightly that maintaining the prosody – in this case the 2-syllable imperative – was more crucial than retaining the precise sense. In German this became "Tu's doch" ("Just do it") and in various other languages the meanings were "Do it!", "Do something!" and "Capture me!" – all of which are good options in the context.

Sometimes a composer takes a line of verse and chops it up with pauses (rests) that produce short phrases of less than 6 syllables. For example a poem by Viau written in French *octosyllabes* begins:

> S'il est vrai, Chloris, que tu m'aimes
> (Mais j'entends que tu m'aimes bien).

But when Reynaldo Hahn set it to music, it emerged thus:

> S'il est vrai – Chloris – que tu m'aimes –
> Mais – j'entends – que tu m'aimes bien –

Each of those en-dashes represents a gap, a rest of an eighth- or a quarter-note. A singable translation of this song will need to replicate the hesitant effect, preferably without suppressing any rests or allowing any word to bridge them.

Let it be noted in passing that the desirable objective of maintaining all the verbal repetitions present in the ST can at times be overruled. If you're not altogether pleased with your version of the phrase – if you have not done justice to the richness of the original – then it is permissible to translate it differently on the second or third occurrence.

In defense of tweaking

Rhythm is certainly an area where "tweaks" (small adjustments) are often possible. Although a perfect translation would retain the original rhythm intact – syllable-count and all stresses – it is unreasonable to insist on this with singable translations. As with any *skopos* involving numerous constraints, you need to claim some flexibility.

A strong justification for tweaking the rhythm is argued, rhetorically, by Arthur Graham: "Don't composers make such changes in setting strophic songs?"

(1989: 34). His point is that they certainly do, indeed they must, whenever the stresses or syllable-count vary from one strophe (verse) to the next. Verse one may start with a single upbeat note, for example, while verse two – though equally octosyllabic – may start with two small upbeat notes and have a slur later in the line. Or two equal notes in one verse may be unequal in the next. Clearly, musicians do not all see the rhythmic details as sacrosanct.

Besides, some strophic texts simply cannot be set to music without such tweaking. When Silcher found this with Heine's "Lorelei" (see chapter 2), he resorted to frequent slurring and even added extra notes in measures 3 and 7. Similarly, when George Gershwin received the text of "Summertime" from the writer Du Bose Heyward, he didn't complain that verse two starts with a 12-syllable line which exceeds the magical 10 syllables of "Summertime and the livin' is easy". Far from requesting a rewrite, Gershwin varied his music slightly, adding a few notes and slurs, and sent the song soaring. It has been recorded hundreds of times.

The conclusion from the above argument is this: *when translators of strophic songs make minor adjustments from verse to verse, they are simply claiming latitudes that are a normal part of songwriting.* This does not apply to hymns, however, or texts intended for ensemble singing by amateur choirs, where uniform syllable-count is highly desirable.

Tweaking the number of notes

Of course it is ideal to maintain the full integrity of the tune, but the difficulties of this task mean that you should not insist on this. Some scholars make much of syllable-count as an issue. They consider that for singing a line of 8 syllables – set to 8 musical notes – must be translated into a line of 8 syllables. Eugene Nida, for example, speaks of "precisely the right number of syllables" (1964: 177). That dogma existed much earlier, of course: it may well explain the willingness of past translators to make elisions not present in current speech (e.g. writing "o'er" instead of "over").

Such an objective is indeed desirable. But in practice a translator who finds that an 8-syllable line is insolubly, unacceptably, clumsy may choose to add a syllable or subtract one. This should be done only in acceptable places, in a filler line (say) rather than a lyrical phrase. And it should be done judiciously. *The best place to add a syllable is on a melisma, and the best place to subtract a syllable is on a repeated note,* because those methods alter rhythm without destroying melody. Joining two repeated notes can be marked on the music score with a tie: a short curved line. Sometimes a little syncopation may be introduced or suppressed. Franzon speaks tolerantly of this kind of tweaking:

> Splitting, merging or adding notes and splitting or creating melismas are minimal ways in which music can be adjusted to fit the lyrics [. . .] If such changes do not affect rhythm or disturb any parallel arrangement of musical phrases, they may be hardly noticed.

(2008: 383–384)

Figure 6.3 Guten Abend (Brahms)

One of his examples shows how a hymn-text in Swedish of 54 syllables was turned into a Finnish text of 62 syllables. This was done chiefly by suppressing almost all the two-note melismas – there was very little tweaking of the melody.

A textbook on translating from German says that with songs: "major compensation is needed throughout the text, specifically to prevent rhythm and rhyme being *foregrounded at the expense of* message content" (italics in original). It then quotes a German song by Wolf Biermann who himself translated it into good English. He repeatedly translated his short isolated word *Kunststück* (2 syllables) as "piece of cake". The syllable-count was clearly not sacrosanct to him (Hervey et al. 2006: 48).

The German phrase "Guten Abend" is routinely translated as "Good evening", which has 3 syllables (normally). When it occurs at the start of Brahms's song "Vergebliches Ständchen" it is given five notes (two slurred together on the long A vowel). The English translators Strangways and Wilson slurred together the first two notes, reducing the 2 syllables of "Guten" to 1. This solved the problem (see Figure 6.3).

Tweaking the melody

Even changes to the melody are not completely out of the question. May not a cautious translator sometimes choose to lose some small melodic detail rather than sacrifice (say) a verbal consideration such as sense or natural word-order? This remark is not meant as a general licence to rewrite melodies, merely as a suggestion that an occasional subtle piece of musical "tweaking" may be preferable to a glaring verbal gaffe. Which is more respectful to the song?

One cannot assume that composers will always be appalled at such liberties. A great master like Mozart, says Harai Golomb, "does not treat his own music and the word-music alignments he so masterfully created, as an infallible and unchangeable holy script" (2005: 136). And the French composer Saint-Saëns, in his *Portraits et souvenirs*, specifically rails against translators who retain every note of a foreign melody, such as the opera-translator who rendered the four-note phrase "Don Giovanni" not as "Don Juan" but as "Don Ju-an-an". "That abomination was unnecessary," said Saint-Saëns. "To avoid it, one needed only to drop a note, instead of respecting wrongly. This kind of respect is the worst of insults. In this matter, as elsewhere, the pedantic letter kills but the spirit gives life" (1900: 239).

Rhythm matters more than rhyme, because rhyme can sometimes be omitted, whereas all songs always have rhythm – indeed all language does. Yet rhyme can be highly desirable, particularly in oral texts like songs (even in languages like English which have largely abandoned rhyme in poetry).

Rhyme – if you really must have it

Although this criterion may be less important than the other four, it has to be factored in from the outset. Why? Because if you add rhyme as an afterthought the results will be awful! Any strategic decision to use rhyme needs to be made early in the process, so that some rhyming-words (the crucial ones) can be found early on. The term "Rhyme" obviously focuses on matching sound-patterns at the end of lines or phrases, especially vowels. These echoes are usually audible and noticed, unless they are separated by at least 20 seconds. Their importance varies from song to song – widely!

The present analysis evaluates rhyme solely in phonetic terms, since that is the objective way to compare them. Thus when we assess "love/dove" as being an excellent rhyme, that merely means excellent in phonetic terms. In non-phonetic terms, actually, we should reject "love/dove" as an odious cliché – but that is rejection on grounds of style and naturalness.

The issue of rhyme has long bedevilled song-translation and has led to many unusable TTs. The underlying problem is poor strategic thinking: consciously or unconsciously many translators have given rhyme a high priority in every song they have attempted. They have usually been mistaken. Some people even seem to think that the mere fact of rhyming confers quality (have they never seen greeting cards?). Rhyming, of course, is difficult: good rhyming seldom happens by accident. Words chosen for sense seldom rhyme. If you find that a rhyming pair has a perfect equivalent (e.g. "eyes/skies" matches the French *yeux/cieux*), then you're just uncommonly lucky!

Does a song-translation absolutely need rhyme? Some translators seem to have assumed, unthinkingly, that rhyme is valued equally everywhere. But really there is no consensus, across languages and cultures, decreeing that rhyme is a necessary component of vocal music. In a TL where songs rhyme seldom or never – such as Japanese – it would be odd to make a rhyming TT. One should instead look at what sort of sound-patterning is actually valued in the oral texts of that target culture – alliterations, extended diphthongs perhaps – and then create a TT using the means of that language to achieve something like what the ST did in the SL.

A good strategy is to ask: "Does my TT need to rhyme at all; is rhyme essential?" You will often answer "desirable, at least." The various reasons why rhyme was deemed desirable in the ST may well apply – to make the song more memorable, more euphonic, more punchy. If the song in question has gusto and wit, then an unrhymed translation will probably disappoint – and actually, some of the words in the ST were chosen *chiefly because they rhymed.*

The pentathlon approach works particularly well in the question of rhyme, because it opposes rigidity of thinking. Where rhyme is present in a ST, some translators simply dispense with it – and in the cases where the rhyme can be lost without much cost, they will be right to do so. In other cases, however, to abandon all rhyme is to score a zero on a really important part of the scorecard. Some other translators will say: "Yes, I will retain rhyme", and will promptly set their target at perfect rhymes as numerous as those in the ST and in the same locations. Sometimes they score very highly, too! But they pay a heavy price in other ways: the rhyme at the end of the line ends up shaping that whole line – the tail wags the dog!

Applying the pentathlon approach, by contrast, will often mean this response: *"Yes, I will have some rhyme. But I will seek some margin of flexibility. In this case the rhymes won't have to be as numerous or as perfect as in the ST, and the original rhyme-scheme need not be observed. I will try to get a top score in Rhyme, but not at too great a cost to other considerations (such as meaning)."*

A good compromise?

Many people have alleged that there is a mistranslation of Shakespeare in Schubert's song "An Sylvia". This song is indeed derived from the lyric "Who is Sylvia?"; and the text that Schubert used, a translation made by Eduard von Bauernfeld, seems to render the original word "kindness" as "Kindheit" ("childhood") – which looks like an elementary error! In defense of the translator, however, we can say that when he confronted a rhyming pair "kindness/blindness", he rendered one noun perfectly ("Blindheit"), and was then led to choose the word "Kindheit", which scores 100 per cent on Rhyme. Of course it doesn't mean "kindness"; but the critics who condemn it on grounds of Sense are mistaken: the word "Kindheit" is not incompatible with the original song – since Sylvia is presumably young, innocent and good. It was a smart trade-off! Overall, Schubert's fine score can count also as a fine Shakespeare setting (and can be actually performed with Shakespeare's ST).

How many rhymes?

This question has not been asked nearly enough. Translators are perhaps too quick to reach for the rhyming dictionary (paperback or online). There is a good article about English versions of Brecht which criticises the song-translations in *Mutter Courage*, saying: "The need to rhyme, moreover, leads to excessive padding" (Lefevere 2000: 240). Surprisingly, however, the author uses the word "need" without asking how much rhyme is really required and fails to question the translators' implicit answer: "As much as was present in the German."

No, song-translations *do not always need as much rhyme* as the ST. Quite often the original song will have about 20 lines of about 8 syllables, all rhyming, often in an ABAB pattern. The TT will naturally want 20 lines of about 8 syllables; but *it will seldom need all of those lines to rhyme.* To score 100 per cent would require

20 rhymes, of course. But it may be acceptable to reduce that number to 10 – with one important proviso: that the word at the end of each verse needs to rhyme with a line earlier in that verse.

With a typical quatrain, a good question to ask is: "Which rhyme-word can I *least afford to lose?*" The answer will usually be the last one, since this is the final word of the semantic unit (the sentence) and of the musical unit (the phrase, ending on a cadence and probably a long note). This desirable "clinching effect" can be achieved with one pair of rhymes, not two. Furthermore, line 4 doesn't have to rhyme with line 2, not if it can easily be rhymed with line 1 or line 3.

And it might not matter whether the other two lines rhyme well – or at all. This is particularly true if the lines are short (if the ST rhymes after every 6 syllables rather than 10 or 12). It is a general rule that the tighter the rhyming, the more the rhyme will determine the whole line.

What about rhyme-scheme?

Many translators in the past have treated rhyme-scheme as a high-priority feature that must not be compromised. But the argument just presented claims that the original rhyme-scheme is seldom crucial to the song. A very common rhyme-scheme for quatrains is ABAB, as in the "Die Lorelei." The most dogmatic view would say that a TT needs two rhyming pairs also, with that same pattern ABAB; and a less dogmatic view would accept the variants AABB and ABBA – also not uncommon in song-lyrics. But an even more flexible view would argue that only one rhyming pair is needed, and that this rhyming pair can be lines 2 and 4 – or it can be lines 1 and 4, or else lines 3 and 4. Admittedly, these options would not score 100 per cent for rhyming. But there are very few songs where listeners actually notice whether the rhyme-scheme is consistent or not.

How perfect should the rhymes be?

To score 100 per cent, you need high-quality rhymes. The usual requirement is that the rhyming words must end with *exactly the same phonemes*, either vowel-consonant or consonant-vowel. (Spelling is irrelevant, because rhyme is phonic in character: "lime" doesn't rhyme with "anime", it rhymes with "thyme".) In addition, *there needs to be similar stress*: in English songs the words "plan" and "Vatican" do not rhyme, since the third syllable of "Vatican" is weak; and "hand" doesn't rhyme with "Finland".

But even where you decide to use rhyme you don't need every rhyme to be perfect. There will probably be places where imperfect rhyme is a good option because it incurs less semantic loss. It was a rigid insistence on perfect rhyme for "love" that opened the window to dozens of "doves" and "stars up above". Except at the end of a stanza, imperfect rhymes such as "move" or "enough" must be deemed acceptable.

Rap music has a lesson here. The vogue for rap performances has reinvigorated rhyme as a technique, at least in English. Rap artists are known for avoiding traditional couplets or quatrains, they can extend a single rhyme for six or twelve lines. The virtuosity is often aided by flexibility: a willingness to accept a word as rhyming merely if the vowel is correct – for example "paid/hate" – or what others might call recourse to partial rhyme (same vowel, adjacent consonant).

A good account of these "partial rhyme" tactics is given by Ronnie Apter, who speaks of "rhyme's cousins – off-rhyme (line-time), weak rhyme (major-squalor), half-rhyme (kitty-knitted) and consonant rhyme (slit-slat) – alone or in combination with other devices like assonance and alliteration" (1985: 309–310). Such devices expand the options for a translator seeking some kind of rhyme or chime, and therefore they reduce the "enslavement to the rhyming dictionary" which has often produced forced or far-fetched TTs. One online dictionary, http://www.rhymezone.com, even offers the option of searching for a "near rhyme". Near-rhymes, incidentally, are available even for allegedly impossible English words like "orange" or "silver". When Herbert Kretzmer translated or adapted *Les Misérables* (the musical by Boublil) he was willing to rhyme "blood" with "God" and "martyrs" with "darkness".

Here is a schema for assessing quality of rhyme, not just in English. Going from rich rhymes (A and G) down to poor near-rhymes (F and L), it seeks to show the range of options without undue complexity.

Options for closed syllables

A. Love/glove   Vowel and the consonants on both sides
B. Love/shove   Good rhyme
C. Love/rough   Final consonant close but not identical
D. Love/move   Vowel close but not identical
E. Love/lug   Final consonant different
F. Love/have   Vowel different

Options for open syllables

G. Belie/rely   Consonant and the vowels on both sides
H. Lie/fly   Good rhyme
I. Lie/rye   Consonant close but not identical
J. Lie/die   Consonant different
K. Lie/lay   Vowel close but not identical
L. Lie/lee   Vowel different

Four of those options are true rhymes (A&G, the richest ones, and B&H). The term "near-rhyme" suits C, D, I and J. We may note that German poets have long accepted cases of option D (*Zeiten/bedeuten* in "Die Lorelei"). As for E and K, they are not good substitutes for rhyme, while F and L can scarcely be heard as kinds of rhyme at all; yet even they may be better than nothing.

How does this chart help the song-translator? In the first place, it greatly widens the pool of available rhyme-words. In the second place, the flexibility offered can lead to better solutions to the other problems: sense, rhythm etc. This plea for tolerance of flexible rhyming is a call to extend the acceptance that has long been given to a few imperfect rhymes (e.g. time/mine in English) to the acceptance of many others – in the interests of overall quality.

One extreme case in English is the word "nothing". As Gene Lees puts it: "*Nothing* rhymes with nothing" (1981: 53). By the above schema, however, near-rhymes like "cutting" and "stuffing" would score quite well, as would all the words that rhyme with them, over twenty words altogether. Look again at the case of "love": English provides only six true rhymes, some of which are problematical – can one use "shove" or "guv"? That is why *songwriters themselves have often settled for near-rhymes*. It follows that song-translators, not being entitled to invent meanings at will as songwriters do, have *even greater reason* to exploit the dozens of near-rhymes available. For "love" there are over twenty in the "rough/stuff" group alone.

A word must be said about so-called feminine rhymes – 2-syllable words where the last syllable is unaccented and the penultimate vowel is the one that needs to rhyme. Also called "trochaic rhymes", these have caused particular problems for song-translators. English poetry makes less use of such endings than poetry in some other languages (such as Italian), and it is often hard to find good rhymes of this kind. Therefore translators working into English need unusual skill in feminine rhymes. One of the easier solutions is to use the "–ing" suffix, but it is boring to overdo this option. Herman and Apter speak of searching for: "syllables such as -es, -le, and -er to match the very light final syllables of words in languages such as German and sung French" (1991: 103). Naturally, their tolerance of imperfect rhymes makes their searching easier. One-syllable rhymes are much easier to find, of course, and so translators sometimes opt to slur the final two notes of the music. Thus, the German *Ich weiss nicht was soll es bedeuten* becomes "I do not know what it can mee-een". This certainly loses points in terms of rhythm. However the need for flexibility can force you to consider this one-syllable option. It is least offensive where the two musical notes are short and on the same pitch.

An extra option for 2-syllable rhymes is to use two words. If you don't want to rhyme "President Putin" with "hi-falutin", you can maybe fall back on "boot in." Comic songs are the best place for such two-word options. Comic songs also allow you to cheat by mispronouncing words. For example: "Have you ever met a boy . . . as clever as oy?" The meaning is clear enough and the rhyme is as perfect as it is silly.

There is also the possibility of changing the location of some rhymes. Traditional poetry can contain "internal rhymes" where you can see the rhyme inside the line:

Young Burt was hurt / When he fell in the dirt

In song, fortunately, rhymes are almost always audible; they are merely more prominent at the end of phrases or on long notes. Song-translators should certainly aim at achieving good sonorities, a sort of generalised "rhyming-ness". To this end, internal or misplaced rhymes can help to compensate in TTs that don't score highly on end-rhymes. Joe Flood showed an example of this in "The Grave-digger" (chapter 5).

Backwards working

Suppose you are translating a rhyming couplet out of English, such as "toes/nose" in this action song for children:

> *Hands, shoulders, knees and toes*
> *and eyes and ears and mouth and nose.*

One good process is to identify the best word to end with, the TL word for "nose" and then do a search on "toes", looking for words that will rhyme – perhaps feet, ankles, shoes, words which though inaccurate do fall in the right semantic field. If this doesn't work, you can do a search on "nose" in the hope of success – perhaps TL words for nostrils, cheeks, face etc. Similarly, for the first quatrain of "Die Lorelei", you should start by translating the last word *Sinn* as "mind" and then hope to find a rhyming word (such as "find") for the end of line 2. With rhyming, work backwards if you can.

Working backwards is working smart: it reduces the chance of the rhyme seeming forced. Consider these lines from Tom Lehrer's 1965 classic "Pollution":

> *Pollution, pollution. You can use the latest toothpaste,*
> *And then rinse your mouth with industrial waste.*

If you were translating this couplet, you should begin with the word "waste". That's how Lehrer worked it: he started with that strong word, hoping to use it as the punch-word at the end of a sentence. Indeed one of the functions of rhyme is to create an expectation and then to deliver a strong rhyming word that clinches both phrase and sentence. Lehrer then looked for a good rhyme to prepare that punch, and the toothpaste hit him in the face. Accordingly you should first find one or two TL options for "industrial waste" and then search through the words that rhyme with it. You would probably not end up with toothpaste, but with luck you'd find a satirical option that was half as good.

Here is a useful overstatement: *half of all rhymes are contrived and unnatural.* A natural word would be produced by some kind of semantic logic, but rhymes are chosen for their sound. In any rhyming pair, the really contrived rhyme is the second one found. In this case it was "toothpaste". But Lehrer cleverly delivered that word first, so that the punch word "waste", when it appeared, sounded right and punchy and perfect. And we can't say that word "waste" was contrived – it was the first of the pair to be found. So here is the conclusion that translators should draw: *try to find your rhyme-words in inverse order*!

Similarly, when W. S. Gilbert wrote the "Major-General's Song" – the one that rhymes "lot o' news" with "hypotenuse" – we can bet that he chose that second rhyme first. Then having found "lot o' news" he gets his Major-General to sing it and then to hesitate ("bothered for a rhyme") before delivering the apparently brilliant "hypotenuse".

Rhyming dictionaries are useful, of course; they are a well-known tool for songwriters. Nearly as useful is the thesaurus – paperback or online – particularly after you know what rhymes you want to use at the end of a line. At that point your draft version of the line may have too many syllables or too few, or perhaps the right number with the wrong stresses. For example when you look up the word "annoyed", you can see a wide semantic field, including words of 2 syllables with trochaic rhythm, and words of 1, 3 or 4 syllables. Andrew Kelly's very practical article advises students, as soon as the rhyme-words are found, to "write them in and compose the line from back to front, like filling in the early letters in a cross-word when the last ones are known" (1992: 92). Thus a draft French translation of that children's action-song might look like this:

Hands, shoulders, knees and toes	*Mains / - - - pieds*
And eyes and ears and mouth and nose.	*Et / - - - / - nez*

The word *pieds* doesn't mean toes, of course, but feet (a superordinate). Yet it works well, and the rhyme is solved. All that remains is to fill in the lines.

The pentathlon approach and its limitations

To conclude this chapter, here is a summary of the "pentathlon principle" as a whole.

Pentathlon principle

When embarking on a singable translation, do not consider that any one feature is sacrosanct and must be retained perfectly. To consider anything sacrosanct *a priori* (either rhyme or metre or shape of phrases or whatever) is to accept a rigid constraint which may lead to great losses. By tolerating some slippage – small margins of compromise in several areas – one can more easily avoid serious translation loss in any single area. A translator working by this principle attempts to score highly in the overall effect of the text, without insisting on unbeatable excellence on any single criterion. With difficult puzzles like this, lateral thinking is required – and lateral thinking requires elbow-room. The more margins of compromise are available, the greater the chance of a successful target text.

A few translators have suggested that this approach lacks rigour, and shows too much willingness to sacrifice verbal and even musical subtleties for the sake of a "user-friendly" TT. The best reply is that the pragmatic compromises involved in song-translating actually cohere with the intrinsic needs of the genre. A song-text is in essence an oral text, not a written one; and the TT is not worth making unless it meets a normal requirement of this *skopos*, namely that it can be understood during performance while the song is sung at the tempo largely predetermined by the composer.

A hexathlon?

The main limitation of this approach lies in a different area: it understates the requirements and constraints of music-drama (musicals, operas etc.). In these genres every song or aria needs to cohere with the extended stage-work that it belongs to, a need not covered by the five criteria expounded above. Perhaps we should identify a sixth criterion with a name like "stage effectiveness" or "dramatic performability" as a separate "event" in what might be a "hexathlon"? If so, we could apply to it all the above strategies of flexibility and trade-offs as ways of finding our solutions – our imperfect, good, workable, even optimal solutions to translating problems.

Except in the matter of surtitling, dramatic vocal music has received little attention in this book; but it is very well covered by major authors on translating for opera, such as Ronnie Apter. One distinctive feature is that the singers are playing roles in a fictional world, performing in character and in costume; they are required to "think what they are singing, to live the lives of the people they are playing on the stage", as a Finnish translator has said (Pullinen 2016). Another feature is that the song-lyrics form a part in the overall storyline and dramatic characterisation. With every musical number we should ask whether the text contains important narrative material or crucial points of interaction with other characters (on stage or off). These requirements may put a special value on particular words and phrases. And the importance of personality encourages contrasts of vocabulary between characters. For example if you are translating the French opera *Carmen* into Chinese or Japanese, you should not give classical aristocratic words to Carmen herself: her register needs to be popular (whereas Don José's language can be more noble, since he considers himself socially superior).

In many operas and musicals there are weaknesses in the overall plot and characters, weaknesses which the translators should be aware of and may try to mitigate. Easier said than done! One Swedish scholar has likened opera-translating to "working in a straitjacket . . . close interrelationships between libretto and music leave little space for movement. Most translation strategies aim at reducing information to gain communication of those features that are considered vital" (Tråvén 2005: 118).

Opera translations, according to one wit, "are like opera plots – all about unfaithfulness." That is an exaggeration. Yet people who think that translating is "all about words" may well form this impression, and that is because they are looking too hard at the actual words and "can't see the forest for the trees". In truth, however, the overall forest matters more. Translating operas and other musicals is more about storyline, character emotion and overall style – the spirit rather than the letter. Perhaps that is why singable versions of operas have sometimes been commissioned from entertaining novelists like Anthony Burgess (*Carmen*) or Roddy Doyle (*Don Giovanni*). An opera translation is a whole work, not an assemblage of phrases or arias.

* * *

Exercise (A) – Rhythm

(a) Invent a song-title in any language consisting of a sentence of eight words at most, a memorable sentence like "The Earth really moves" or "Smoke gets in your eyes." Imagine that this sentence will be sung six times as a refrain.

(b) Then translate it into another language in such a way that the TT rhythm is the same as the ST rhythm. To gauge your success, invent a melodic phrase that fits and then sing your two versions to that music. (Who knows: this could develop into a bilingual song!)

Exercise (B) – Syllables

When you want a singable translation, you seek (ideally) to devise a TT with the same number of syllables, and with the stresses on the right syllables. Try to translate this line from the Beatles ("Eleanor Rigby"): "wearing the face that she keeps in a jar by the door."

There are 13 syllables, one to each word, with strong beats on syllables 1, 4, 7, 10 and 13. Whatever the TL, you should try to have the same stresses and syllable-count to match the tune.

Exercise (C) – Translate into rhyming verse

Too many songs have short lines and frequent rhymes! Here's the start of Peter Low's "Panda Song":

> We leased a panda for the zoo,
> a giant panda from Gansu.
> And what did he do?
> He ate bamboo.
> He was a photogenic sight
> in classic fuzzy black-and-white.
> And what did he do?
> He ate bamboo.

Make a singable translation, trying to keep to the English syllable-count, but giving priority to the rhymes.

Or, if you find this exercise too difficult, try to explain what exactly the difficulties are.

Exercise (D) – Major translation exercise

Look again at the song-lyric printed in chapter 1, "Older Ladies" by Donnalou Stevens. This humorous piece makes the serious point that women don't have to be young to be attractive and fun. The music has a lively bluegrass or country style featuring banjos, yet the entertainment comes chiefly from the words.

View it on YouTube (just Google "Donnalou Older Ladies"), and you'll note how the words "older ladies" sound rather like "yodelaydeez", and that the vocal line suddenly leaps up high in a sort of yodel, in imitation of Tyrolean Jodelmusik. This play on words is reinforced by images of people wearing Lederhosen in an Austrian meadow. How could one replicate that?

Attempt nevertheless to make a singable translation! Try both to be faithful to the ST and to create a TT which a performer would perform successfully (with or without the videoclip).

Exercise (E) – *Messiah*

The words for this well-known oratorio are extracts from the King James Version of the *Bible* (a version whose translators were enjoined to produce a text suitable for reading aloud in church). The complete text can be found on http://opera.stanford.edu/iu/libretti/messiah.htm

1   Select one of the solos in it, and listen to the opening line or two.
2   Note closely to how the composer has set it: tune, rhythm, downbeats.
3   Compare it with the same *Bible* verse in your other language.
4   Try to adapt that verse to make it fit the existing music.

For example line one of "He shall feed his flock" has 10 syllables with strong beats on 2, 5 and 9. The setting is syllabic except for two notes on "shall" and a five-note melisma on syllable 9. The melody is gentle and fairly slow (a *siciliano*).

Further reading

The topics of rhythm and rhyme in singable translations are addressed in almost all the readings suggested in chapter 6, notably in articles by Apter and Hermann, and by Franzon.

The present chapter has reworked material in Low, Peter (2008) "Translating Songs that Rhyme" in *Perspectives* 16, 1/2: 1–20.

The following readings specifically concern OPERA and MUSICALS:

Apter, Ronnie (1985) "A Peculiar Burden: Some Technical Problems of Translating Opera for Performance in English" in *Meta* 30/4: 19–28.

Gorlée, Dinda (1997) "Intercode Translation: Words and Music in Opera" in *Target* 9/2: 235–270.

Herman, Mark & Apter, Ronnie (1991) "Opera Translation", in Larson, M. (ed) *Translation, Theory and Practice, Tension and Interdependence*, Binghampton, State University of New York, 100–119.

"The Impossible Takes a Little Longer" (1989) in *Translation Review* 30/31: 21–37.

Irwin, Michael (1996) *Translating Opera*, Exeter, Elm Bank.
"Questions of Quality" (1989a) in *Ars Lyrica* 4: 19–28.
Gorlée (2005) contains four very relevant articles, those by Tråvén, Golomb, Apter and Herman, and Franzon.

References

Apter, Ronnie (1985) "A Peculiar Burden: Some Technical Problems of Translating Opera for Performance in English" in *Meta* 30/4: 309–319.

Franzon, Johan (2005) "Musical Comedy Translation" in Gorlée (2005).

Franzon, Johan (2008) "Choices in Song Translation" in *The Translator* 14/2: 373–399.

Golomb, Harai (2005) "Music-linked Translation [MLT] and Mozart's Operas" in Gorlée (2005), 121–162.

Gorlée, Dinda (ed) (2005) *Song and Significance: Virtues and Vices of Vocal Translation*, Amsterdam & New York, Rodopi.

Graham, Arthur (1989) "A New Look at Recital Song Translation" in *Translation Review* 29, 31–37.

Herman, Mark & Apter, Ronnie (1991) "Opera Translation" in Larson (1991).

Hervey, S., Loughridge, M. & Higgins, I. (2006) *Thinking German Translation*, London & New York, Routledge.

Kelly, Andrew (1992) "Translating French Song as a Language Learning Activity" in *Traduire et interpréter Georges Brassens* (1992–1993), a collective volume from the Institut Supérieur de Traducteurs et Interprètes, Bruxelles.

Larson, M. (ed) (1991) *Translation, Theory and Practice, Tension and Interdependence*, Binghampton, State University of New York.

Lees, Gene (1981) *The Modern Rhyming Dictionary*, New York, Cherry Lane.

Lefevere, André (2000) "Mother Courage's Cucumbers", in Venuti, L. (ed) *The Translation Studies Reader*, London & New York, Routledge, 233–249.

Nida, Eugene (1964) *Toward a Science of Translating*, Leiden, Brill.

Palmer, Judi (2012) "Surtitling Opera: A Surtitler's Perspective", in Minors, Helen (ed), *Music, Text and Translation*, London, Bloomsbury.

Pullinen, Erkki (2016, March 22) Personal communication.

Saint-Saëns, C. (1900) *Portraits et souvenirs*, Paris, Société d'éditions artistiques.

Tråvén, Marianne (2005) "Musical Rhetoric – The Translator's Dilemma" in Gorlée (2005).

7   The place of adaptations

The option of deviating from fidelity

Translations or adaptations?

Although this is a "How-To" book about translating songs, its advice differs from the actual practices that many song-translators have followed. Whereas this book has said: "Try to make close translations", many translators seem to have often proceeded from the injunction: "Don't translate, adapt". Yet if the approach outlined here seems hostile to adaptations, that is mostly because it has focused on actually solving translation difficulties – whereas adaptors can choose to avoid them.

Adaptation is indeed one way of carrying songs across language borders. This book has generally used the word "translation" in the sense accepted by translators, which requires close transfer of meaning between languages. But not always: it has ventured, especially in chapters 5 and 6, beyond the field of close transfer (the core of most translating work), in order to cope with untypical source-texts and unusual *skopoi*. Besides, many derivative song-texts mentioned above are not close translations at all. Indeed some people choose to take a broad definition, for example Gideon Toury for whom "a 'translation' will be taken to be any target-language utterance which is presented or regarded as such" (1995: 20). That kind of "external definition" of translations suits his descriptive study purposes.

This book, however, prefers an internal definition, one which will help to distinguish a translated text from an adapted one. Failure to distinguish adaptations from translations would condemn us to unfocused discussions about disparate cases, "mixing apples with pears". Yet if we accept that "there is a point at which adaptation ceases to be translation at all" (Bastin 1998: 6), then we can propose that a TT, if it is be called "a translation", needs to be faithful to the ST in many respects, including transfer of meaning. This assumption follows what could be called the "Fidelity Paradigm", a paradigm being a set of ideas about how something should be done or thought about. The Fidelity Paradigm centres on the expectation that a TT should respect the ST and the original author behind it.

Most translators care about Fidelity – we try to replicate in the TL what the ST did in the SL, we try to recreate it without dominating or distorting it. We weigh up every word in a text. We never claim that the TT is our own creation, rather we see ourselves as serving the work and its author and its purpose . . . not trying to impose ourselves on it. We are modest intermediaries, and we do not shout: "Look at me!" (a temptation we resist with quiet pride). The Fidelity Paradigm applies in various other fields too – to restorers of old paintings, to cooks carefully following the recipe of a master chef, or to classical musicians performing the works of the great composers. These are experts with whom we can be pleased to align ourselves. Anyone who calls such an approach easy or uncreative is mistaken.

Yet we live in a culture where a different approach is widely followed, which could be termed the Adaptation Paradigm. When people retell jokes, they often alter the wording. When people rewrite folktales like *Cinderella*, they assume that even outrageous changes are OK. In TV and cinema, screen versions of novels or plays or even biographies do not merely transpose the medium: a few dare to impose happy endings, and most of them ignore or change significant details, including details that could easily have been transferred. This Adaptation Paradigm is dominant in jazz and popular music, where pre-existing songs are "covered" by later singers. Although the performers are not actually compelled to alter much – except perhaps the pitch to suit their voices – they often choose to do so, even when the original was excellent. Sometimes there is extensive adaptation, without justification: one adaptor even tackled the lively song "America" from *West Side Story* and ditched the *guajira* rhythm, a distinctive alternation between 6/8 and 3/4 especially chosen for singing by Puerto Ricans. Yet this was not a parallel to the tale of *Cinderella* which belongs to everyone and no one; this was the specific creation of Sondheim and Bernstein. (The fact that the public liked the adapted version is irrelevant, because the piece was a travesty: the singer should have invented his own music in flat-footed 4/4 instead of trampling on someone else's.)

Song-lyrics too are subject to adaptation, of course, particularly when they cross language borders. Some singable versions of popular music that are called "translations" are really freely adapted; and some TTs are not called translations at all: the published sheet music at times says "English lyric by . . .", as a clear alternative to "English translation by . . ."

This difference may be important. When Klaus Kaindl analysed the handling in Germany of Edith Piaf's song "Hymne à l'amour" (music by Marguerite Monnot), he found that the German TT by Michael Kunze was accepted by many listeners in Germany and Austria as "genuine Piaf in translation". Yet Kaindl enumerates various ways in which Kunze toned down the text and thereby incorporated it better into the German subgenre of "Schlager". And that is not all: he insists that those changes were not forced ones and proves this point by citing an alternative German TT (Kaindl 2013). The version by Ina Deter is less domesticated, and conveys more of the very French *môme Piaf* – her emotional intensity, her gritty realism and her tragic sense. Some may say that the weaknesses of Kunze's adaptation don't matter, provided the audiences were happy. But fans of Piaf may well insist that Kunze's version had sold those audiences short – or at least that "adaptation" was the correct way to describe it.

Songwriters too might deem it important to call adaptations by that name. They created the original lyrics, after all, and we cannot assume they will be indifferent to what happens to them. At least some songwriters are resentful when they judge another version of their creative work to be a travesty or betrayal, or when they hear a distortion being presented as a good representation of their songs.

Besides, there are legal issues of intellectual property, and so lawyers may find the distinction important too. The music industry is wealthy, and there is money in copyrights. Yet here's a strange observation: musicians working with vocal music from past centuries – music in the public domain – are generally more concerned about authenticity and respect than musicians working with recent songs. Classical music inclines toward the Fidelity Paradigm, even with music over 300 years old. Popular music is more anarchic and takes liberties even with songs which, under the Berne Convention, will remain under copyright for decades to come.

The best way to examine the difference between translations and adaptations is by focusing on Sense, the matter of verbal meaning. Here are two proposed definitions:

A translation is a TT where all significant details of meaning have been transferred.

An adaptation is a derivative text where significant details of meaning have not been transferred which easily could have been.

These are distinguishing definitions which offer a practical litmus test: to apply it one simply compares the actual wording of ST and the TT. Both translation and adaptation draw on the ST, but only one has wilfully modified it. A typical adaptation mixes genuine transfer with forms of unforced deviation (omission, addition, modification), it "draws on an ST but has extensively modified it for a new cultural context" (Munday 2009: 166).

It is true that the notions of "significant details" and "unforced changes" may permit different people to classify particular changes differently. But this is deliberate – and it usefully identifies two points about which, in some cases, opinions may diverge. For example some people tend to view instances of "domestication" (see chapter 4) as normal and forced, whereas others see them as unnecessary and easily avoided. Naturally, the notion of "unforced deviation" excludes normal changes in word-order, or the other standard procedures outlined in textbooks and used regularly by good translators, such as those termed "transposition" and "modulation" (Vinay & Darbelnet 1958: 55).

To some purists, these two definitions err by tolerating TTs which take liberties with insignificant details, and not refusing to call them translations. But some extension to the term is surely needed: in song-translating compromises and trade-offs are not optional but essential. The phrase "easily could have been" is actually meant to excuse some omissions and modifications made by "singable translators", by offering this defence: "Given the constraints of the *skopos*, there was no easy way for me to transfer that detail. If you want to prove that I've made a bad translation, or a non-translation, you will have to show that it could easily be improved." Additions are harder to defend, however. Supposing a song purporting to be a translation contains a distinctive phrase (such as "night birds" or "slice of heaven") with no counterpart in the ST. Even if that phrase is one that works well, the process that produced it was not translating, but creative lyric-writing.

Let's apply these definitions to a well-known round (four-part canon), beginning with the original French, but omitting the repeats:

(A) *Frère Jacques, dormez-vous?*
Sonnez les matines, din din don.

This is sometimes sung in English with these words:

(B) "Are you sleeping, Brother John?
Ring the bell for mattins, ding ding dong."

Is example (B) a translation? It puts the man's name last, and renders Jacques as John. Does that matter? No, the French word-order is certainly not significant. Nor is the name "John", although "James" or "Jack" would be closer. What about the bells, shouldn't they be plural? That is not certain, and "Ring the bells for mattins" includes a nasty consonant-cluster LZF. We can conclude that (B) qualifies as a translation.

What about this version?

(C) "Brother Jacko, are you dead?
Did an apple hit you on the head?"

This text is clearly derivative, yet it makes numerous changes, obviously wilful. It is indeed a parody – and parodies are always adaptations.

What of this version, which actually rhymes?

(D) "In the forest, there are trees.
Johnny saw a squirrel, and some bees."

Although it fits perfectly the well-known music, it is neither a translation of (A) nor an adaptation. The rhythm is the same, obviously, and this text can fit the likely purpose of group singing. *But it is not a derivative text at all.* It was invented – not derived – by the music-first pattern. A useful term for this is "replacement text".

Interlude: Replacement texts

These are song-lyrics where the music is recognisably the same as an earlier song, but where the words manifest no semantic transfer from the ST, even though the lyric has been created to match that same music, especially its rhythm.

A clever example is "The Elements" by Tom Lehrer: "There's antimony, arsenic, aluminum, selenium . . ." The music comes from the Gilbert and Sullivan operetta *The Pirates of Penzance* (1879). But the words are not an intralingual translation of Gilbert's words, or even an adaptation. They transfer nothing whatever from the text of the "Major-General's Song". Instead they replace them. Lehrer simply took Sullivan's music, and worked on the music-first pattern which many songwriters use. The true ST was actually the Periodic Table!

Similarly, "Twinkle, twinkle little star" is not a translation of "Ah, vous dirai-je, maman" (or vice versa): it is a different song with the same tune. The reason why it cannot be considered the same song is the lack of a semantic connection. The "Sukiyaki Song" is not a translation or adaptation of the Japanese "Ue o Muite Aruko" (which made no reference to hot food): it is a replacement text. As for the texts created from unintentional or deliberate mishearing of a foreign language (sometimes called "soramimi"), these may be amusing, but they are not translations.

Making replacement texts can be compared to what songwriters Sherman and Busch did in 1964, when they created the hit song "Hello Mother, Hello Father". They took an old instrumental tune (by Ponchielli) and gave it words about a boy at summer camp. In doing so, they were following the music-first pattern. Their song was certainly not a translation or adaptation: indeed there was no ST at all, unless you count one real boy's real letter sent home from his holiday. (Later, its success prompted real translations or adaptations from their English text, into Swedish for example.)

Replacement texts are far from rare. Popular song-tunes from the US receive completely new texts in China, and English rock-songs trigger Russian versions in which "the meaning is completely altered" (McMichael 2008: 213). One reason for making replacement texts is obvious: someone sees merit in an existing song-tune but finds the lyric weak, trite or silly, and so feels impelled to write better words. This is an interesting cultural phenomenon. It may involve the wish for an international audience, as when the Polish group Coma released an album of their existing songs with rewritten English lyrics having nothing in common to their Polish original lyrics. But it is not translating: it is "non-translating". And if the singers who perform such texts call them translations, then they are lying and misleading the audience. In some cases replacement texts are written by people quite incapable of translating, for example the many English lyrics sung in the 1940s to the popular melody "Lili Marleen" – lively and vulgar lyrics devised by British and US soldiers who knew no German but liked the catchy tune.

This interlude about replacement texts scarcely belongs in a book about translating. It is included in order to insist that some songs which are claimed or believed to be translations or adaptations do not qualify, whatever their merits may be – and also to promote the term "replacement texts" as an aid to talking about this phenomenon.

Adaptations

For that German song "Lili Marleen", there was also a standard and competent English version. Yet in the classic 1961 film *Judgement at Nuremberg* the character played by Marlene Dietrich criticises this version as being very inaccurate. And she is correct: it is clearly an adaptation as defined in this chapter. This case is not at all uncommon. For example Paul Anka took the song "Comme d'habitude" (by Claude François) and made the man's character much prouder in his English version "My Way", later recorded by Sinatra. The song "Waterloo Road" (Jason Crest) was so altered by Joe Dassin that it became "Aux Champs-Élysées", with all traces of London erased. Such alterations mean that, for close analysis at least, the term "translation" is too inaccurate for these cases, whereas "adaptation" fits well, because it accommodates the practice of making omissions, additions or modifications for a certain new cultural situation.

A student in Ireland, Seán Ó Luasa, has remarked that: "adaptation may simply just present the easiest option: it is manifestly less difficult than translation, and using the ST lyrics as inspiration is arguably less creatively taxing than the production of a replacement text" (2014: 29). He is right. Imagine a crossword clue that said: "Find any good 8-letter word that fills this gap". Wouldn't that be easier than a normal clue with only one solution? Similarly, the search for "an impressive 8-syllable line to fit this musical phrase" becomes easier if meaning is deemed irrelevant or unimportant. We must concede, however, that excellent adaptations are also creatively taxing – especially if they result in amusing parodies.

But ease is only one of many factors. A more conscious consideration is the desire to communicate well with a TL audience. This applies especially to adaptations made by popular singers, who constantly wish to strike some chord with their audiences. Many of them desire to amuse, to startle, even to woo their fans. Some of their techniques, understandably, involve unforced changes, for example domesticating the place-names of a song.

In some cases these adaptors never sought much fidelity in the first place, like the film-director who allegedly made a movie of *The Grapes of Wrath* without reading Steinbeck's novel. A successful British rock-song, for example, may form just the starting-point for a significantly different song in Russian, nevertheless presented as a song by (say) Robbie Williams. One may wonder at the ethics of this. Would it not be more honest to the Russian songwriter to start from scratch? And would not the original songwriter(s) have reason to resent this treatment?

One may wonder also at the legality of it. Suppose that the well-known song "Where Have All the Flowers Gone?" (Pete Seeger) was recorded in a Spanish version, with permission, and made a lot of money. Suppose then that the songwriter's lawyers noticed that the verbal chain in the song (flowers ⇒ young girls ⇒ soldiers ⇒ graveyards ⇒ flowers) had not survived in this Spanish version. They might then take this to court arguing that the circularity of this chain is an essential feature, "the very DNA of the song", and that any translation which destroys it is a travesty, an insult (and that they had heard Seeger's ghost shouting at midnight: "They are trampling on my song!"). They would certainly declare it unethical to present the recording as "A translation of Seeger's song". And it is possible that they would win a case for breach of copyright.

That case is imaginary. A real case did occur in 1970, concerning a prose work. The Czech writer Kundera saw that an English translation of his first novel had omitted sections and even transposed chapters. He complained and seems to have

threatened legal action, with strong justification. Any writer, as a later commenta-
tor put it, "remains a key participant in any action that involves a text which still
bears his name, and as such is entitled to be treated with dignity and respect: his
consent should have been sought for such a major form of intervention" (Baker
2011: 283). At one point Kundera himself angrily likened such manipulation to
home-invasion: "This is my house not yours!" (Margala 2010: 30).

A note about legality

Something must be said here about copyright matters. These vary between
jurisdictions, and this book is not competent to give legal advice. But the
general truth can be stated, based on the Berne Conventions: *songs and
song-lyrics are the intellectual property of their creators*. They do not enter
the "public domain" until many years after the creator's death. The usual
figure in the UK and the EU is 70 years; in the US it is often 95 years
from publication, or else covers everything after 1923. (No wonder this
book quoted many songs from before 1920 – for which no permission was
needed.) A good website giving advice on the subtleties of US copyrights is
http://copyright.cornell.edu/resources/publicdomain.cfm.

One does, of course, encounter many recent songs and lyrics posted
online. But most of these postings are unauthorised, and sometimes a website is asked or compelled to remove them on legal grounds, or to pay for
the right. Artists recording "covers" of recent popular songs have to pay
royalties to use them. And you cannot assume that creators don't care what
happens to their work. A pop-singer who posts her lyrics on her own website is certainly not surrendering ownership of them.

So if you plan to use other people's work, especially for financial gain,
you are advised to seek permission.

In other cases, however, translators do seek to respect a source, and yet still fail
to achieve fidelity. This may lead them to change direction and turn to adapting. Consider this account from Joe Flood, concerning the *chansons* of Georges
Brassens:

> I started with as literal a translation as I could make rhyme, then I treated that
> as I would a rough draft of one of my own lyrics and tailored it to the melody.
> Then I went back and tried to make sure it was at least in the spirit of the
> original and adjusted where I could.

He goes on to say: "I think adaptation is probably a more accurate description"
(Flood 2010). This account indicates some deliberate shifts of focus during the
process: taking the literal meaning from the ST, finding rhymes, matching the
draft TT to the melody, comparing this draft with the original, and making adjustments to better match its "spirit". As a translator-performer, Joe Flood wanted

to achieve two simultaneous outcomes: a TT that he could sing with conviction himself, and a total song that remained very much a work of Brassens.

This book has not been called "How to Adapt Songs". Yet it assumes that in the future, as in the past, a lot of songs will be adapted. This last chapter even suggests a recipe: *To adapt a song, first try to translate it, and later – if you realise you have failed – transform your draft translation into an adaptation that works well in the TL.* Then at least something of the original song will have crossed the language border.

Besides, most people will concede that some song-translations do have substantial success in transferring every significant detail of a song from one language to another. Such versions deserve to be performed and enjoyed, though not of course at the expense of the SL originals.

* * *

Perhaps we can conceive of the whole corpus of vocal music in many languages as a "World Heritage Park" – a huge cultural playground separate from the nearby park devoted to instrumental music. This "Song Park" contains many wonderful treasures. Some are well known, others are hard to find, and opinions differ widely about what its greatest treasures are. But in this park we can surely see an important role for a particular kind of "tour-guide services", those that are provided by skilful and sensitive language specialists – translators.

Exercise (A) – Translation or adaptation?

1   Write a critique of this singable TT, comparing it with the prose TT below in italics (or with the German original).

This TT completely fails to follow the ST rhyme-scheme. But how many partial rhymes and internal rhymes can you count? Do they compensate for the poor rhyming? Are there plenty of long vowels?

Various details (<u>underlined</u> in the prose TT) seem to be absent from the singable version. It has ignored line 13 completely. Is this is a serious weakness? Would you call this a translation or an adaptation?

And what if anything could justify the word "thief" in line 4?

Die nacht

Aus dem Walde tritt die Nacht,
Aus den Bäumen schleicht sie leise,
Schaut sich um im weitem Kreise,
    Nun gib acht.
Alle Lichter dieser Welt,
Alle Blumen, alle Farben
Löscht sie aus und stiehlt die Garben
    Weg vom Feld.

Alles nimmt sie, was nur hold,
Nimmt das Silber weg des Stroms,
Nimmt vom Kupferdach des Doms
    Weg das Gold.
Ausgeplündert steht der Strauch,
Rücke näher, Seel an Seele;
O die Nacht, mir bangt, sie stehle
    Dich mir auch.

Night

Night emerges from the trees,
from the forest dark and leafy,
gazes round the day-lit landscape
    like a thief,
Ev'ry brightness of the world,
ev'ry colour, ev'ry flower
Night will steal, and ev'ry grain-stack
    from the field.
Night comes coldly raiding all,
takes the silver from the stream
and from off the gleaming dome
    peels the gold.
Nothing fair remains to see.
Come and hold me near and tightly
for I fear that Night may steal
    you away from me.

Out of the woods steps Night, out from the trees she sneaks softly, looks about in a wide circle; now beware!
All the lights of this world, all the flowers, all the colours she extinguishes, and steals the sheaves from the field.
She takes everything that is lovely; takes the silver from the stream; from the cathedral's copper roof she takes the gold.
The shrubs stand plundered; draw nearer, soul to soul; oh, I fear that Night will also steal you from me.

2   German-English students will be able to examine its relation to the ST more closely. It is by H. von Gilm, and the best-known setting, by R. Strauss, can be heard at http://www.youtube.com/watch?v=wV9m5XgTvdw

Exercise (B) – Translation, adaptation, or what?

For Chinese-English students

1   Consider the song "Let It Go" by Demi Lovato. It has been claimed that the Chinese version sung by Bella Yao is a close translation. But do you think

that this has omitted or altered some important elements that could have easily been retained?

2   Consider the song "Lemon Tree" by Fool's Garden. It has been claimed that the Chinese lyric sung by Tarcy Su bears no resemblance to the ST. Would you call this a "replacement text" or a free adaptation?

For Japanese-English students

Consider the song "My Grandfather's Clock" (written in 1876 by Henry Clay Work). It has been claimed that the Japanese version sung by Ken Hirai is a close translation. But do you think that this has omitted or altered some important elements, such as the lines: "It was taller by half than the old man himself / Though it weighed not a pennyweight more"?

Exercise (C) – An early English songwriter

FAIR, IF YOU EXPECT ADMIRING, by Thomas Campion, 1601

Fair, if you expect admiring,
Sweet, if you provoke desiring,
    Grace dear love with kind requiting.
Fond, but if thy sight be blindness,
False, if thou affect unkindness,
    Fly both love and love's delighting.
Then when hope is lost and love is scorned
I'll bury my desires, and quench the fires
That ever yet in vain have burned.

Fates, if you rule lovers' fortune,
Stars, if men your powers importune,
    Yield relief by your relenting.
Time, if sorrow be not endless,
Hope made vain, and pity friendless,
    Help to ease my long lamenting.
But if griefs remain still unredressed,
I'll fly to her again and sue for pity
To renew my hopes distressed.

Campion, a contemporary of Shakespeare, wrote in Elizabethan English. The word "burned" was sounded as 2 syllables. Here is a paraphrase in modern English:

Pretty woman, if you expect to be admired, sweetie, if you make men desire you, then reward my precious love by generously returning it.
But if, dear one, you are blind, or if, false woman, you show rejection, then flee from love and love's delights.
In that case, when my hope is lost and my love is scorned, I'll bury my desires and extinguish the fires of passion that so far have burned in vain.

Fair, if you expect admiring.

Poem and music by
THOMAS CAMPION
1601.

Fates, if you rule lover's fortune,
Stars, if men your powers importune,
  Yield relief by your relenting.
Time, if sorrow be not endless,
Hope made vain, and pity friendless,
  Help to ease my long lamenting.
But if griefs remain still unredressed,
  I'll fly to her again and sue
  For pity to renew
  My hopes distressed.

Figure. 7.1 "Fair, if you expect admiring" (Campion), music

You Fates, if you rule lovers' fortunes, you Stars, if your powers make men's lives difficult, then relent and grant me relief from your harshness.

Oh Time, unless sorrow must be endless and hope futile and pity hostile, then help to ease my long lamenting.

But if my grievances are still not redressed, I'll fly to her again and beg her to pity me so as to renew my frustrated hopes.

This is a strophic song with a short repeat but no refrain. The rhymes near the end of verse two appear in a different position from those in verse one.

Melismas are not numerous; a translation could perhaps add more. As for the music, the simple tune features slow notes in measures 5–6 and fast notes in measures 12 and 14. It is enhanced by an accompaniment written originally for lute (which can be played on guitar, harpsichord or other keyboard instrument). The key may seem to be G major, but it isn't really, as the various F naturals attest.

Attempt to make a singable translation or adaption into another language, or an intralingual translation into twenty-first-century English.

Exercise (D) – Fidelity?

In the context of literary translating, it is not surprising to read assertions like this:

1 "The translator must always be faithful to his original, and he has no right whatever to take liberties with it. He is a translator, not an editor, not a paraphraser, nor a populariser. Nor has he any right to try to smooth the reader's path by the omission of 'dull' bits, short-circuitings, explanatory additions, radical transferences or changes of order" (Tancock 1978: 24–25).

2 "The translation should be a faithful rendition of the work into English: it shall neither omit anything from the original text nor add anything to it other than such verbal changes as are necessary in translating into English" (*A Handbook for Literary Translators*, 2nd ed, New York, PEN American Center, 1991, 16).

Are the above statements absolutely true of all literary translation?

Are they true only when the text is a recognised classic?

Do they remain true after the text has entered the public domain?

Are they true of recent popular songs, which have not become classics (though are under copyright)?

Are they true when the "explanatory additions" merely provide details that the original audience already knew and didn't need to be told?

Exercise (E) – Copyright

If you were interested in a recent song recorded in your country and wanted to see who held the copyright, how would you go about finding out? Try some Internet searches!

And if was an older song, an American song from the 1930s, could you find out whether it is now in the public domain?

Figure 7.2 "Im schwarzen Walfisch", music

Exercise (F) – Translate or adapt

Chapter 3 gave the German words of the song entitled "Altassyrisch", along with a prosaic "study translation". Every verse begins "Im schwarzen Walfisch".

Attempt a singable translation of this song, so as to fit the traditional music given in Figure 7.2.

An English translator can find the first rhyming pair easily enough, from the cognate words *Tag* and *Lag*. But the other rhymes will prove harder.

Rather than translating, you may instead choose to adapt the song, replacing the ST's playful references to the ancient world with something else, for example a Sci-Fi setting in a Ferengi bar.

Further reading

This chapter has reworked and developed some of the material in Low, Peter (2013) "When Songs Cross Language Borders: Translations, Adaptations and 'Replacement Texts'" in *The Translator* 19/2: 229–244.

References

Baker, M. (2011) *In Other Words*, Oxford & New York, Routledge.

Bastin, G. (1998) "Adaptation", in M. Baker (ed) *Routledge Encyclopedia of Translation Studies*, 1st edition, London & New York, Routledge, 5–8.

Flood, J. (2010, June) Personal communication.

Kaindl, K. (2013) "From Realism to Tearjerker and Back: The Songs of Edith Piaf in German", in Minors, H. (ed) *Music, Text and Translation*, London & New York, Bloomsbury, 151–161.

Margala, M. (2010) "The Unbearable Torment of Translation" in *Transcultural* 1/3: 30–42.

McMichael, P. (2008) "Translation, Authorship and Authenticity in Soviet Rock Songwriting" in *The Translator* 14/2: 201–228.

Munday, J. (ed) (2009) *The Routledge Companion to Translation Studies*, London & New York, Routledge.

Ó Luasa, S. (2014) "Case Study: A Survey and Translation Quality Assessment of Popular Music Translated" unpublished thesis, Dublin City University.

PEN American Center (1991) *A Handbook for Literary Translators*, 2nd edition, New York.

Tancock, L. (1978) Preface to Lafayette *The Princesse de Cleves*, Harmondsworth, Penguin.

Toury, G. (1995) *Descriptive Translation Studies and Beyond*, Amsterdam, Benjamins.

Vinay, J.P. & Darbelnet, J. (1958) *Stylistique comparée du français et de l'anglais*, Paris, Didier.

Glossary

Adaptation   This book defines an adaptation as a derivative text where significant details of meaning have not been transferred which easily could have been.

Aria   This Italian word refers to the major solo numbers in operas and oratorios. An aria is often preceded by a **recitative**, which is less melodic and more conversational.

Chanson   This French word for song denotes particularly the popular song tradition represented by Piaf, Brassens, Ferré, Aznavour and others. By contrast, French "art songs" are often called *mélodies*.

Communicative translation   This means a reader-friendly TT which (in Newmark's terminology) focuses more on communicating with the audience than on close fidelity to the ST.

Downbeat   The strongest regular beat in a piece of music, which standard notation places just after the barline. When there is a single note just before the barline it is called the **upbeat.**

Explicitation   Making explicit some information that was merely implied in the ST.

Gist translation   A précis TT that transfers only the most important elements of the ST.

Gloss translation   A wordy TT that includes notes and explanations.

Harmony   The chords, all the notes sounded at one moment. Choice of harmony and chord-progression often enhances a song's emotional "colour".

Lexicon   Vocabulary, store of words.

Lied   This German word for song (plural *Lieder*) is sometimes used in the narrower sense of "Art song in the nineteenth-century tradition of Schubert". Yet it can go far beyond German examples: the LiederNet archive contains texts and translations of highbrow songs from dozens of countries.

Logocentric   Word-centred. This book applies the term "logocentric" to songs where the words are more important than the music. Generally, however, songs tend to be musico-centric.

Melisma   Two or more notes all sung on one syllable. For example the first syllable of "Silent Night" or the "-ot" syllable in "Swing Low Sweet Chari-ot".

Melody   The tune. The notes the singer sings, rising and falling in pitch.

Metre The basic time-structure of a piece of music. Waltzes, for example, are in triple metre, whether they are slow or fast. The most common metre in European music is quadruple: four beats to the bar, for which the time-signature is 4 over 4, meaning 4 quarter-notes in every measure.

Metronome marking A metronome is a device to give precise indication of tempo (= speed). The marking ♩ = 80 on a piece of printed music tells us the unit counted (in this case the quarter-note or crotchet ♩) and the number of those units per minute.

Musico-centric This book applies the term "musico-centric" to songs where the music is more important than the words.

Naturalness Naturalness, in a translation, means that a native speaker of the TL judges that the text could have been created spontaneously in that language.

Neologism Newly invented word or phrase.

Partial rhyme (also called "near-rhyme" or "slant rhyme") Word-pairs like "time/mine" where the final sounds have some resemblance, usually in the vowels, but not enough to make them true rhymes (which require either same vowel and following consonant or same consonant and following vowel).

Phonic Concerning the sounds of words and not their sense.

Recitative In operas and oratorios, especially in Italian, recitatives are wordy sections which the singer declaims, with prescribed pitch but no clear rhythm or melody.

Refrain The verbal phrases that are repeated more than once after every verse of a strophic song. When a group of people join in, the refrain is literally "the chorus".

Register The variety of language chosen, especially its degree of formality.

Semantic This adjective means "concerning the meaning of words". A "semantic translation" (in Newmark's terminology) focuses more on fidelity to the ST than on making things easy for the audience.

Sense The meaning of the words, the content, what they are pointing to.

Singability The term is used here to mean "relative ease of vocalisation". It focuses on the physical action of singing.

Skopos This Greek word, meaning "purpose or aim", is used in books about translation to designate the "goal or purpose, defined by the commission and if necessary adjusted by the translator" (see reference in chapter 3: Vermeer 1989: 230). Thinking about *skopos* (plural *skopoi*) helps translators to clarify their objectives and select appropriate strategies.

SL Source language.

Slur The curved mark on a musical score indicating a melisma (two or more notes on one syllable).

ST Source text.

Strophic A song comprising several verses ("strophes") all sung to the same tune.

Surtitles Captions projected above the stage, notably in opera, thus different from film subtitles, which are projected low down on the screen.

Syllabic setting   A text is "set syllabically" where every syllable corresponds to one note of music (i.e. there are no melismas).

Tempo   In music, this term means speed.

Through-composed   A term calqued on the German *durchkomponiert*. In a through-composed song every line of text has its own tune, unlike a strophic song where the same music is repeated for several verses.

Tie   A curved mark on a musical score joining two notes at the same pitch.

TL   Target language.

Trochaic   This concerns the rhythm of a word like "crazy". It is trochaic because its 2 syllables have a strong-weak rhythm (stressed followed by unstressed, and often also long then short).

TT   Target text.

Index